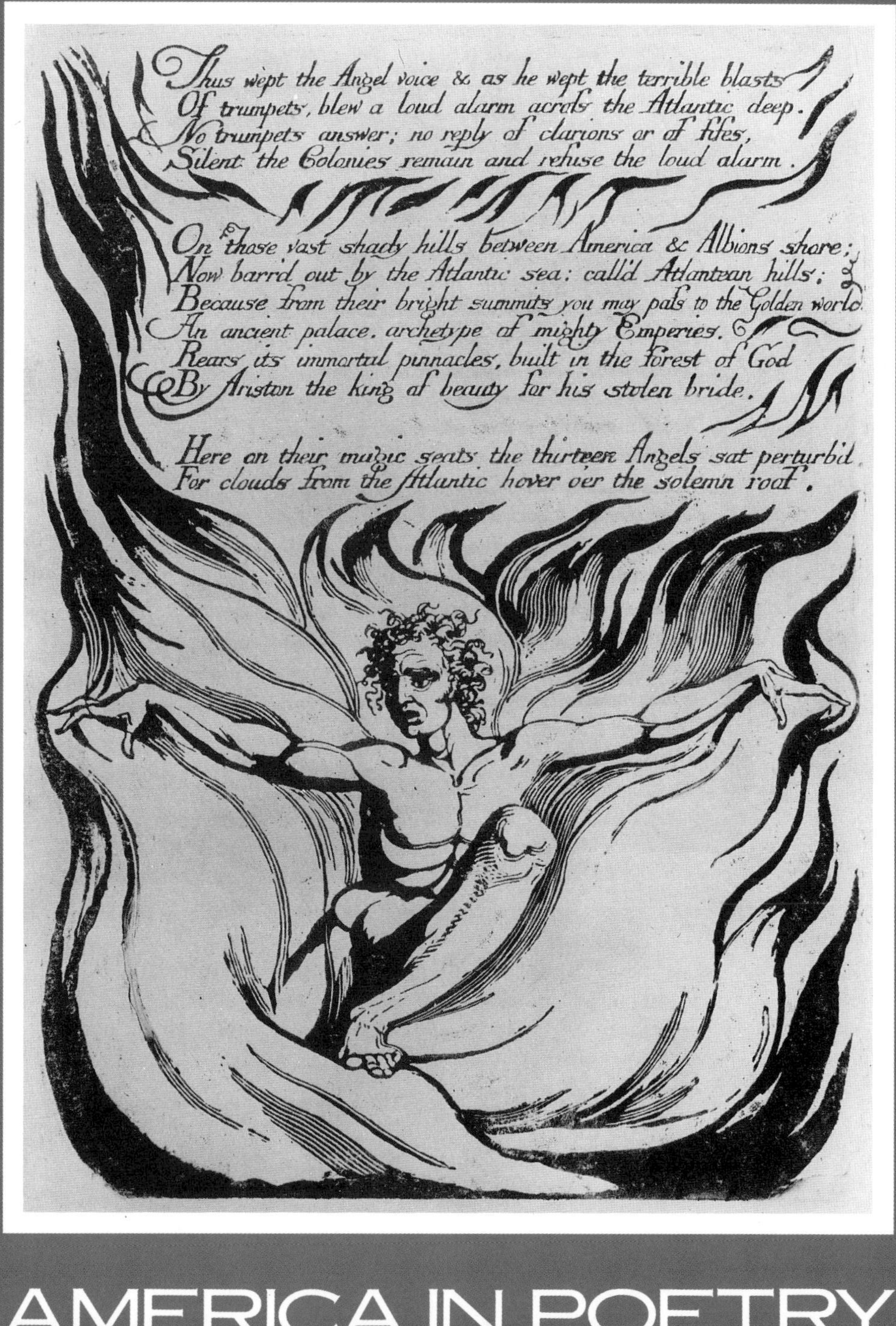

AMERICA IN POETRY

MY COUNTRY NEED NOT CHANGE HER GOWN

Emily Dickinson

My country need not change her gown,
Her triple suit as sweet
As when 'twas cut at Lexington,
And first pronounced "a fit."

Great Britain disapproves, "the stars";
Disparagement discreet,—
There's something in their attitude
That taunts her bayonet.

AMERICA IN POETRY

WITH PAINTINGS, DRAWINGS, PHOTOGRAPHS,
AND OTHER WORKS OF ART

EDITED BY
CHARLES SULLIVAN

HARRY N. ABRAMS, INC., PUBLISHERS, NEW YORK

Editor: *Lois Brown*
Designer: *Carol A. Robson*
Rights and Reproductions: *J. Susan Sherman*

Library of Congress Cataloging-in-Publication Data
America in poetry.
  Includes bibliographies and indexes.
  1. American poetry.   2. English poetry.   I. Sullivan,
Charles, 1933–
PS584.A38   1988   811'.008   88-3337
ISBN 0-8109-1880-3

*The type for this book was set and cast
at the Out of Sorts Letter Foundery
in Monotype's Deepdene.*

Half-title page: Plate 10 in *America a Prophecy* by William Blake,
1793. *Library of Congress*

*Title page: Liberty in the Form of the Goddess of Youth,
giving support to the Bald Eagle in front of the Trenton Arches.*
About 1800–15. Silk embroidery, watercolor,
sequins, and mica on silk.
DAR Museum, Washington, D.C.

A Times Mirror Company

Printed and bound in Japan

CONTENTS

TO THE READER

"America is hard to see," said Robert Frost, and I agree. America is so big, so complicated, and in some ways so frequently changing, that none of us can see this country as a whole. Pictures help, but there is more to "seeing" America than what we can see with our eyes. We use our other senses, too, and beyond them, we imagine, we remember, we think about things, and we have feelings—love of country, concern for the future, curiosity about the past. And we do all this as individuals, so that my "America" is different from yours, and both are different from someone else's.

Poetry helps us to grasp these sensations, thoughts, and emotions beyond what our eyes can see. John Holmes, a twentieth-century poet who lived in Massachusetts most of his life, wrote:

> On my own map of my own country
> I shall show where there were never wars,
> And plot the changed way I hear men speak in the west,
> Words in the south slower, and food different.

But most poets stay closer to home; they write about what they know best—the sights, the sounds, the smells, as well as the thoughts and feelings that these things arouse in them. Although some American poetry is panoramic, much of it consists of "close-ups" through which poets share their personal experiences with us.

This book brings together more than a hundred poems, ranging from the panoramic to the very personal, about many different aspects of American life—the colonies, the Revolution, westward exploration, later wars, friends and family, life in our cities and towns, and so on. Together with the poems, I have included paintings, drawings, and photographs that echo or enhance the poetry in one way or another. Some of these works of art are so beautiful or striking that, at first glance, you may think this is an "art book" with poetry added. As you examine it more carefully, however, I hope you will see that the poems are the heart of the book.

I did not think of trying to represent America in poetry until I was middle-aged. Poetry I had encountered since childhood, but it took many years, many travels and experiences, for me to know America well enough to realize that various poems could be brought together into a kind of mosaic or composite of this country. It is my own selection. You might choose different poems; someone else might select others. But all of us would probably have certain choices in common, such as "Old Ironsides," "Snow-bound," or "The Gift Outright."

Several of the poems have a special importance to me. For example, I went to high school with Sylvia Plath, and I met Valerie Worth at Swarthmore. The poets John Ciardi and Robert Hillyer were judges of poetry contests that I won. I grew up with the poetry of Robert Frost, but what I remember most vividly is hearing him read "The Road Not Taken" in 1960 (give or take a year) at the YMHA in Manhattan. When he came to the last lines of that poem, he paused until the large audience was breathlessly silent, and then continued, almost in a whisper:

> I shall be telling this with a sigh
> Somewhere ages and ages hence:
> Two roads diverged in a wood, and I—
> I took the one less traveled by,
> And that has made all the difference.

Many of us took such roads in the sixties, for one reason or another. Mine led me away from poetry and "literary" interests for a long time, but closer to America. Now I am getting back to all that—even writing poems again myself—and one of the results is this book, which gives me joy I'd like to share with you.

Of all those who helped to make *America in Poetry* possible, three people at Abrams deserve special thanks: Paul Gottlieb, my friend and publisher, for giving me the opportunity to create a different kind of book; Lois Brown, editor, for guiding me through the creative process with wisdom and good humor; and Carol Robson, designer, for producing a thing of beauty that will be a joy forever.

CHARLES SULLIVAN
WASHINGTON, D.C.

Robert Frost

America Is Hard to See

Columbus may have worked the wind
A new and better way to Ind
And also proved the world a ball,
But how about the wherewithal?
Not just for scientific news
Had the Queen backed him to a cruise.

Remember he had made the test
Finding the East by sailing West.
But had he found it? Here he was
Without one trinket from Ormuz
To save the Queen from family censure
For her investment in his venture.

There had been something strangely wrong
With every coast he tried along.
He could imagine nothing barrener.
The trouble was with him the mariner.
He wasn't off a mere degree;
His reckoning was off a sea.

And to intensify the drama
Another mariner, da Gama,
Came just then sailing into port
From the same general resort,
And with the gold in hand to show for
His claim it was another Ophir.

Had but Columbus known enough
He might have boldly made the bluff
That better than da Gama's gold
He had been given to behold
The race's future trial place,
A fresh start for the human race.

He might have fooled Valladolid.
I was deceived by what he did.
If I had had my chance when young
I should have had Columbus sung
As a god who had given us
A more than Moses' exodus.

Terre de la Floride.
Manuscript map dated 1555
by the French pilot and hydrographer
Guillaume Le Testu.
Musée de la Marine, Paris

But all he did was spread the room
Of our enacting out the doom
Of being in each other's way,
And so put off the weary day
When we would have to put our mind
On how to crowd but still be kind.

For these none-too-apparent gains
He got no more than dungeon chains
And such small posthumous renown
(A country named for him, a town,
A holiday) as, where he is,
He may not recognize for his.

They say his flagship's unlaid ghost
Still probes and dents our rocky coast
With animus approaching hate,
And for not turning out a strait,
He has cursed every river mouth
From fifty North to fifty South.

Someday our navy, I predict,
Will take in tow this derelict
And lock him through Culebra Cut,
His eyes as good (or bad) as shut
To all the modern works of man
And all we call American.

America is hard to see.
Less partial witnesses than he
In book on book have testified
They could not see it from outside—
Or inside either for that matter.
We know the literary chatter.

Columbus, as I say, will miss
All he owes to the artifice
Of tractor-plow and motor-drill.
To naught but his own force of will,
Or at most some Andean quake,
Will he ascribe this lucky break.

High purpose makes the hero rude;
He will not stop for gratitude.
But let him show his haughty stern
To what was never his concern
Except as it denied him way
To fortune-hunting in Cathay.

He will be starting pretty late.
He'll find that Asiatic state
Is about tired of being looted
While having its beliefs disputed.
His can be no such easy raid
As Cortez on the Aztecs made.

THIS NEWLY CREATED WORLD

Winnebago (Anonymous)

Pleasant it looked,
this newly created world.
Along the entire length and breadth
of the earth, our grandmother,
extended the green reflection
of her covering
and the escaping odors
were pleasant to inhale.

Effigy bowl.
Winnebago bowl made of oak, mid-19th century.
Denver Art Museum

11

TO THE VIRGINIAN VOYAGE

Michael Drayton

You brave heroic minds,
Worthy your country's name,
That honor still pursue,
Go and subdue,
Whilst loitering hinds
Lurk here at home, with shame.

Britons, you stay too long:
Quickly aboard bestow you,
And with a merry gale
Swell your stretch'd sail,
With vows as strong
As the winds that blow you.

Your course securely steer,
West and by south forth keep!
Rocks, lee-shores, nor shoals,
When Eolus scowls,
You need not fear,
So absolute the deep.

And cheerfully at sea,
Success you still entice,
To get the pearl and gold,
And ours to hold
Virginia,
Earth's only paradise.

Where nature hath in store
Fowl, venison, and fish,
And the fruitful'st soil,
Without your toil,
Three harvests more,
All greater than your wish.

And as there plenty grows
Of laurel everywhere,—
Apollo's sacred tree,—
You it may see,
A poet's brows
To crown, that may sing there.

from
POCAHONTAS

William Makepeace Thackeray

Wearied arm, and broken sword
Wage in vain the desperate fight;
Round him press a countless horde,
He is but a single knight.
Hark! a cry of triumph shrill
Through the wilderness resounds,
As, with twenty bleeding wounds,
Sinks the warrior, fighting still.

Now they heap the funeral pyre,
And the torch of death they light;
Ah! 'tis hard to die by fire!
Who will shield the captive knight?
Round the stake with fiendish cry
Wheel and dance the savage crowd,
Cold the victim's mien and proud,
And his breast is bared to die.

Who will shield the fearless heart?
Who avert the murderous blade?
From the throng with sudden start
See, there springs an Indian maid.
Quick she stands before the knight:
"Loose the chain, unbind the ring!
I am daughter of the king,
And I claim the Indian right!"

Dauntlessly aside she flings
Lifted axe and thirsty knife,
Fondly to his heart she clings,
And her bosom guards his life!
In the woods of Powhatan
Still 'tis told by Indian fires
How a daughter of their sires
Saved a captive Englishman.

Pocahontas (later known as Rebecca Rolfe).
Painted in England about 1616. Oil on canvas.
National Portrait Gallery, Smithsonian Institution.
Gift of Andrew W. Mellon, 1942

WHY WHY SHOULD I
THE WORLD BE MINDING

Thomas Smith

Why why should I the World be minding
therin a World of Evils Finding.
 Then Farwell World: Farwell thy Jarres
  thy Joies thy Toies thy Wiles thy Warrs
Truth Sounds Retreat: I am not Sorye.
 The Eternall Drawes to him my heart
 By Faith (which can thy Force Subvert)
To Crown me (after Grace) with Glory.

Self Portrait by Thomas Smith.
17th century. Oil on canvas.
The poem in the painting
appears on the opposite page.
Worcester Art Museum, Massachusetts

from
THE PILGRIM FATHERS

William Wordsworth

Well worthy to be magnified are they
Who, with sad hearts, of friends and country took
A last farewell, their loved abodes forsook,
And hallowed ground in which their fathers lay;
Then to the new-found World explored their way,
That so a Church, unforced, uncalled to brook
Ritual restraints, within some sheltering nook
Her Lord might worship and his word obey
In freedom. Men they were who could not bend;
Blest Pilgrims, surely, as they took for guide
A will by sovereign Conscience sanctified;
Blest while their Spirits from the woods ascend
Along a Galaxy that knows no end,
But in His glory who for Sinners died.

From Rite and Ordinance abused they fled
To Wilds where both were utterly unknown;
But not to them had Providence foreshown
What benefits are missed, what evils bred,
In worship neither raised nor limited
Save by Self-will. Lo! from that distant shore,
For Rite and Ordinance, Piety is led
Back to the Land those Pilgrims left of yore,
Led by her own free choice. So Truth and Love
By Conscience governed do their steps retrace.—
Fathers! your Virtues, such the power of grace,
Their spirit, in your Children, thus approve.
Transcendent over time, unbound by place,
Concord and Charity in circles move.

from
THE COURTSHIP OF MILES STANDISH

Henry Wadsworth Longfellow

In the Old Colony days, in Plymouth the land of the Pilgrims,
To and fro in a room of his simple and primitive dwelling,
Clad in doublet and hose, and boots of Cordovan leather,
Strode, with a martial air, Miles Standish the Puritan Captain.
Buried in thought he seemed, with his hands behind him, and pausing
Ever and anon to behold his glittering weapons of warfare,
Hanging in shining array along the walls of the chamber,—
Cutlass and corselet of steel, and his trusty sword of Damascus,
Curved at the point and inscribed with its mystical Arabic sentence,
While underneath, in a corner, were fowling-piece, musket, and matchlock.
Short of stature he was, but strongly built and athletic,
Broad in the shoulders, deep-chested, with muscles and sinews of iron;
Brown as a nut was his face, but his russet beard was already
Flaked with patches of snow, as hedges sometimes in November.
Near him was seated John Alden, his friend and household companion,
Writing with diligent speed at a table of pine by the window;
Fair-haired, azure-eyed, with delicate Saxon complexion,
Having the dew of his youth, and the beauty thereof, as the captives
Whom Saint Gregory saw, and exclaimed, "Not Angles, but Angels."
Youngest of all was he of the men who came in the Mayflower.

Pilgrims Going to Church *by George Henry Boughton.*
1867. Oil on canvas.
The New-York Historical Society, New York City

Gravestone of Joseph Tapping, 1678.
King's Chapel, Boston.
(Photograph by Daniel Farber)

GO THEN, MY DOVE, BUT NOW NO LONGER MINE

Cotton Mather

Go then, my DOVE, but now no longer *mine;*
Leave *Earth,* and now in *heavenly Glory* shine,
Bright for thy Wisdome, Goodness, Beauty here;
Now *brighter* in a more *angelick Sphaere.*
JESUS, with whom thy Soul did long to be,
Into His *Ark,* and Arms, has taken thee.
Dear *Friends,* with whom thou didst so dearly live,
Feel thy *one Death* to *them* a *thousand* give.
Thy *Prayers* are done; thy *Alms* are spent; thy *Pains*
Are *ended* now, in *endless* Joyes and Gains.
    I faint, till thy last Words to Mind I call;
    Rich Words! HEAV'N, HEAV'N WILL MAKE AMENDS FOR ALL.

HERE FOLLOWES SOME VERSES UPON THE BURNING OF OUR HOUSE, JULY 10TH, 1666.

Anne Bradstreet

In silent night when rest I took,
For sorrow neer I did not look,
I waken'd was with thundring nois
And Piteous shreiks of dreadfull voice.
That fearfull sound of fire and fire,
Let no man know is my Desire.

I, starting up, the light did spye,
And to my God my heart did cry
To strengthen me in my Distresse
And not to leave me succourlesse.
Then coming out beheld a space,
The flame consume my dwelling place.

And, when I could no longer look,
I blest his Name that gave and took,
That layd my goods now in the dust:
Yea so it was, and so 'twas just.
It was his own: it was not mine;
Far be it that I should repine.

He might of All justly bereft,
But yet sufficient for us left.
When by the Ruines oft I past,
My sorrowing eyes aside did cast,
And here and there the places spye
Where oft I sate, and long did lye.

Here stood that Trunk, and there that chest;
There lay that store I counted best:
My pleasant things in ashes lye,
And them behold no more shall I.
Under thy roof no guest shall sit,
Nor at thy Table eat a bitt.

No pleasant tale shall 'ere be told,
Nor things recounted done of old.
No Candle 'ere shall shine in Thee,
Nor bridegroom's voice ere heard shall bee.
In silence ever shalt thou lye;
Adeiu, Adeiu; All's vanity.

Then streight I 'gin my heart to chide,
And did thy wealth on earth abide?
Didst fix thy hope on mouldring dust,
The arm of flesh didst make thy trust?
Raise up thy thoughts above the skye
That dunghill mists away may flie.

Thou hast an house on high erect,
Fram'd by that mighty Architect,
With glory richly furnished,
Stands permanent though this bee fled.
It's purchased, and paid for too
By him who hath enough to doe.

A Prise so vast as is unknown,
Yet, by his Gift, is made thine own.
Ther's wealth enough, I need no more;
Farewell my Pelf, farewell my Store.
The world no longer let me Love,
My hope and Treasure lyes Above.

RESENTMENTS COMPOSED BECAUSE OF THE CLAMOR OF TOWN TOPERS OUTSIDE MY APARTMENT

Sarah Kemble Knight

I ask thy Aid, O Potent Rum!
To charm these wrangling Topers Dum.
Thou hast their Giddy Brains possest—
The man confounded with the Beast—
And I, poor I, can get no rest.
Intoxicate them with thy fumes:
O still their Tongues till morning comes!

Embroidered chair seat cover attributed to Anne Bradstreet.
17th century. Colored wool embroidered on cotton and linen twill.
Museum of Fine Arts, Boston. Gift of Samuel Bradstreet

Home of Anne Bradstreet,
North Andover, Massachusetts.
Engraving, 19th century.
The New York Public Library

OF SCOLDING WIVES AND THE THIRD DAY AGUE

Henricus Selyns

Among the greatest plagues, one is the third day ague;
    But cross and scolding wives the greatest evil are;
With strong and pray'rful minds the first will cease to plague you,
But for the last I know not what advice to dare;
    Except with patience all to suffer,
    And ne'er the first assault to proffer.

19

ON THE PROSPECT OF PLANTING ARTS AND LEARNING IN AMERICA

George Berkeley

The Muse, disgusted at an age and clime
    Barren of every glorious theme,
In distant lands now waits a better time,
    Producing subjects worthy fame:

In happy climes where from the genial sun
    And virgin earth such scenes ensue,
The force of art by nature seems outdone,
    And fancied beauties by the true:

In happy climes, the seat of innocence,
    Where nature guides and virtue rules,
Where men shall not impose for truth and sense
    The pedantry of courts and schools:

There shall be sung another golden age,
    The rise of empire and of arts,
The good and great inspiring epic rage,
    The wisest heads and noblest hearts.

Not such as Europe breeds in her decay;
    Such as she bred when fresh and young,
When heavenly flame did animate her clay,
    By future poets shall be sung.

Westward the course of empire takes its way;
    The four first acts already past,
A fifth shall close the drama with the day;
    Time's noblest offspring is the last.

speeches from
THE RISING GLORY OF AMERICA

Hugh Henry Brackenridge and Philip Freneau

Eugenio

   'Tis true no human eye can penetrate
The veil obscure, and in fair light disclos'd
Behold the scenes of dark futurity;
Yet if we reason from the course of things,
And downward trace the vestiges of time,
The mind prophetic grows and pierces far
Thro' ages yet unborn. We saw the states
And mighty empires of the East arise
In swift succession from the Assyrian
To Macedon and Rome; to Britain thence
Dominion drove her car, she stretch'd her reign
O'er many isles, wide seas, and peopled lands.
Now in the west a continent appears;
A newer world now opens to her view.

She hastens onward to th' Americ shores
And bids a scene of recent wonders rise.
New states, new empires and a line of kings,
High rais'd in glory, cities, palaces,
Fair domes on each long bay, sea, shore or stream,
Circling the hills now rear their lofty heads.

Leander

   And here fair freedom shall forever reign.
I see a train, a glorious train appear,
Of patriots plac'd in equal fame with those
Who nobly fell for Athens or for Rome.
The sons of Boston, resolute and brave,
The firm supporters of our injur'd rights,
Shall lose their splendors in the brighter beams
Of patriots fam'd and heroes yet unborn.

The Bermuda Group by John Smibert.
1729. Oil on composition board.
Dean Berkeley stands at the right;
the artist pictured himself at the far left.
Yale University Art Gallery,
New Haven. Gift of Isaac Lothrop

UNHAPPY BOSTON

Paul Revere

Unhappy Boston! see thy sons deplore
Thy hallowed walks besmear'd with guiltless gore.
While faithless Preston and his savage bands
With murderous rancor stretch their bloody hands;
Like fierce barbarians grinning o'er their prey,
Approve the carnage and enjoy the day.
If scalding drops, from rage, from anguish wrung,
If speechless sorrows lab'ring for a tongue,
Or if a weeping world can aught appease
The plaintive ghosts of victims such as these;
The patriot's copious tears for each are shed,
A glorious tribute which embalms the dead.
But know, Fate summons to that awful goal,
Where justice strips the murderer of his soul:
Should venal C——ts, the scandal of the land,
Snatch the relentless villain from her hand,
Keen execrations on this plate inscrib'd
Shall reach a judge who never can be bribed.

PAUL REVERE'S RIDE

Henry Wadsworth Longfellow

Listen, my children, and you shall hear
Of the midnight ride of Paul Revere,
On the eighteenth of April, in Seventy-five;
Hardly a man is now alive
Who remembers that famous day and year.

He said to his friend, "If the British march
By land or sea from the town tonight,
Hang a lantern aloft in the belfry arch
Of the North Church tower as a signal light—
One, if by land, and two, if by sea;
And I on the opposite shore will be,
Ready to ride and spread the alarm
Through every Middlesex village and farm,
For the country folk to be up and to arm."

Then he said, "Good-night!" and with muffled oar
Silently rowed to the Charlestown shore,
Just as the moon rose over the bay,
Where swinging wide at her moorings lay
The Somerset, British man-of-war;
A phantom ship, with each mast and spar
Across the moon like a prison bar,
And a huge black hulk, that was magnified
By its own reflection in the tide.

Meanwhile, his friend, through alley and street,
Wanders and watches with eager ears,
Till in the silence around him he hears
The muster of men at the barrack door,
The sound of arms, and the tramp of feet,
And the measured tread of the grenadiers,
Marching down to their boats on the shore.

The Ride of Paul Revere by Grant Wood.
1931. Oil on masonite.
The Metropolitan Museum of Art.
Arthur Hoppock Hearn Fund.
Copyright Estate of Wood/V.A.G.A., New York, 1986

Then he climbed the tower of the Old North Church,
By the wooden stairs, with stealthy tread,
To the belfry-chamber overhead,
And startled the pigeons from their perch
On the sombre rafters, that round him made
Masses and moving shapes of shade—
By the trembling ladder, steep and tall,
To the highest window in the wall,
Where he paused to listen and look down
A moment on the roofs of the town,
And the moonlight flowing over all.

Beneath, in the churchyard, lay the dead,
In their night-encampment on the hill,
Wrapped in silence so deep and still
That he could hear, like a sentinel's tread,
The watchful night wind, as it went
Creeping along from tent to tent,
And seeming to whisper, "All is well!"
A moment only he feels the spell
Of the place and the hour, and the secret dread
Of the lonely belfry and the dead;
For suddenly all his thoughts are bent
On a shadowy something far away,
Where the river widens to meet the bay—
A line of black that bends and floats
On the rising tide, like a bridge of boats.

Meanwhile, impatient to mount and ride,
Booted and spurred, with a heavy stride
On the opposite shore walked Paul Revere.
Now he patted his horse's side,
Now gazed at the landscape far and near,
Then, impetuous, stamped the earth,
And turned and tightened his saddle-girth;
But mostly he watched with eager search
The belfry-tower of the Old North Church,
As it rose above the graves on the hill,
Lonely and spectral and sombre and still.
And lo! as he looks, on the belfry's height
A glimmer, and then a gleam of light!
He springs to the saddle, the bridle he turns,
But lingers and gazes, till full on his sight
A second lamp in the belfry burns!

A hurry of hoofs in a village street,
A shape in the moonlight, a bulk in the dark,
And beneath, from the pebbles, in passing, a spark
Struck out by a steed flying fearless and fleet;
That was all! And yet, through the gloom and the light,
The fate of a nation was riding that night;
And the spark struck out by that steed, in his flight,
Kindled the land into flame with its heat.

He has left the village and mounted the steep,
And beneath him, tranquil and broad and deep,
Is the Mystic, meeting the ocean tides;
And under the alders that skirt its edge,
Now soft on the sand, now loud on the ledge,
Is heard the tramp of his steed as he rides.

It was twelve by the village clock
When he crossed the bridge into Medford town.
He heard the crowing of the cock
And the barking of the farmer's dog,
And felt the damp of the river fog
That rises after the sun goes down.

It was one by the village clock
When he galloped into Lexington.
He saw the gilded weathercock
Swim in the moonlight as he passed,
And the meeting-house windows, blank and bare,
Gaze at him with a spectral glare,
As if they already stood aghast
At the bloody work they would look upon.

It was two by the village clock
When he came to the bridge in Concord town.
He heard the bleating of the flock
And the twitter of birds among the trees,
And felt the breath of the morning breeze
Blowing over the meadows brown.
And one was safe and asleep in his bed
Who at the bridge would be first to fall,
Who that day would be lying dead,
Pierced by a British musket-ball.

You know the rest. In the books you have read,

How the British Regulars fired and fled—
How the farmers gave them ball for ball
From behind each fence and farm yard wall,
Chasing the red-coats down the lane,
Then crossing the fields to emerge again
Under the trees at the turn of the road,
And only pausing to fire and load.

So through the night rode Paul Revere;
And so through the night went his cry of alarm
To every Middlesex village and farm—
A cry of defiance and not of fear,
A voice in the darkness, a knock at the door,
And a word that shall echo forevermore!
For, borne on the night-wind of the Past,
Through all our history, to the last,
In the hour of darkness and peril and need,
The people will waken and listen to hear
The hurrying hoof-beats of that steed,
And the midnight message of Paul Revere.

CONCORD HYMN

Ralph Waldo Emerson

By the rude bridge that arched the flood,
Their flag to April's breeze unfurled,
Here once the embattled farmers stood,
And fired the shot heard round the world.

The foe long since in silence slept;
Alike the conqueror silent sleeps;
And Time the ruined bridge has swept
Down the dark stream which seaward creeps.

On this green bank, by this soft stream,
We set to-day a votive stone;
That memory may their deed redeem,
When, like our sires, our sons are gone.

Spirit that made those heroes dare
To die, and leave their children free,
Bid Time and Nature gently spare
The shaft we raise to them and thee.

The Bloody Massacre (at Boston, March 5th, 1770).
Engraving, 1770, by Paul Revere
after a drawing by Henry Pelham.
Library of Congress

TO THE MEMORY

*Of the brave Americans, under General Greene, in South Carolina,
who fell in the action of September 8, 1781*

Philip Freneau

At Eutaw springs the valiant died:
Their limbs with dust are cover'd o'er—
Weep on, ye springs, your tearful tide;
How many heroes are no more!

If in this wreck of ruin, they
Can yet be thought to claim a tear,
O smite thy gentle breast, and say
The friends of freedom slumber here!

Thou, who shalt trace this bloody plain,
If goodness rules thy generous breast,
Sigh for the wasted rural reign;
Sigh for the shepherds, sunk to rest!

Stranger, their humble graves adorn;
You too may fall, and ask a tear:

'Tis not the beauty of the morn
That proves the evening shall be clear—

They saw their injur'd country's woe;
The flaming town, the wasted field;
Then rush'd to meet the insulting foe;
They took the spear—but left the shield,

Led by thy conquering genius, GREENE,
The Britons they compell'd to fly:
None distant view'd the fatal plain,
None griev'd, in such a cause, to die—

But, like the Parthian, fam'd of old,
Who, flying, still their arrows threw;
These routed Britons, full as bold,
Retreated, and retreating slew.

Now rest in peace, our patriot band;
Though far from Nature's limits thrown,
We trust, they find a happier land,
A brighter sun-shine of their own.

LIBERTY AND PEACE, A POEM

Phillis Wheatley

Lo! Freedom comes. Th' prescient Muse foretold,
All Eyes th' accomplish'd Prophecy behold:
Her Port describ'd, "*She moves divinely fair,*
Olive and Laurel bind her golden Hair."
She, the bright Progeny of Heaven, descends,
And every Grace her sovereign Step attends;
For now kind Heaven, indulgent to our Prayer,
In smiling *Peace* resolves the Din of *War.*
Fix'd in *Columbia* her illustrious Line,
And bids in thee her future Councils shine.
To every Realm her Portals open'd wide,
Receives from each the full commercial Tide.
Each Art and Science now with rising Charms
Th' expanding Heart with Emulation warms.
E'en great *Britannia* sees with dread Surprize,
And from the dazzl'ing Splendor turns her Eyes!
Britain, whose Navies swept th' *Atlantic* o'er,
And Thunder sent to every distant Shore:
E'en thou, in Manners cruel as thou art,
The Sword resign'd, resume the friendly Part!
For *Galia's* Power espous'd *Columbia's* Cause,
And new-born *Rome* shall give *Britannia* Law,
Nor unremember'd in the grateful Strain,
Shall princely *Louis'* friendly Deeds remain;
The generous Prince th' impending Vengeance eye's,
Sees the fierce Wrong, and to the rescue flies.
Perish that Thirst of boundless Power, that drew
On *Albion's* Head the Curse to Tyrants due.
But thou appeas'd submit to Heaven's decree,
That bids this Realm of Freedom rival thee!
Now sheathe the Sword that bade the Brave atone
With guiltless Blood for Madness not their own.
Sent from th' Enjoyment of their native Shore.
Ill-fated—never to behold her more!
From every Kingdom on *Europa's* Coast
Throng'd various Troops, their Glory, Strength
and Boast.

With heart-felt pity fair *Hibernia* saw
Columbia menac'd by the Tyrant's Law:
On hostile Fields fraternal Arms engage,
And mutual Deaths, all dealt with mutual Rage;
The Muse's Ear hears mother Earth deplore
Her ample Surface smoak with kindred Gore:
The hostile Field destroys the social Ties,
And ever-lasting Slumber seals their Eyes.
Columbia mourns, the haughty Foes deride,
Her Treasures plunder'd, and her Towns destroy'd:
Witness how *Charlestown's* curling Smoaks arise,
In sable Columns to the clouded Skies!
The ample Dome, high-wrought with curious Toil,
In one sad Hour the savage Troops despoil.
Descending *Peace* and Power of War confounds;
From every Tongue celestial *Peace* resounds:
As for the East th' illustrious King of Day,
With rising Radiance drives the Shades away,
So Freedom comes array'd with Charms divine,
And in her Train Commerce and Plenty shine.
Britannia owns her Independent Reign,
Hibernia, Scotia, and the Realms of *Spain;*
And great *Germania's* ample Coast admires
The generous Spirit that *Columbia* fires.
Auspicious Heaven shall fill with fav'ring Gales,
Where e'er *Columbia* spreads her swelling Sails:
To every Realm shall *Peace* her Charms display,
And Heavenly *Freedom* spread her golden Ray.

PHILLIS WHEATLEY, NEGRO SERVANT to Mr. JOHN WHEATLEY, of BOSTON.

Published according to Act of Parliament, Sept.ʳ 1, 1773 by Arch.ᵈ Bell, Bookseller Nᵒ. 8 near the Saracens Head Aldgate.

Frontispiece for an English edition
of Phillis Wheatley's poems.
Engraving, 1773.
National Portrait Gallery,
Smithsonian Institution

from
ODE RECITED AT THE
HARVARD COMMEMORATION

James Russell Lowell

I praise him not; it were too late;
And some innative weakness there must be
In him who condescends to victory
Such as the Present gives, and cannot wait,
   Safe in himself as in a fate.
     So always firmly he:
     He knew to bide his time,
     And can his fame abide,
Still patient in his simple faith sublime,
    Till the wise years decide.
  Great captains, with their guns and drums,
    Disturb our judgment for the hour,
      But at last silence comes;
These all are gone, and, standing like a tower,
Our children shall behold his fame,
The kindly-earnest, brave, foreseeing man,
Sagacious, patient, dreading praise, not blame,
New birth of our new soil, the first American.

Girl with portrait of Washington.
Daguerreotype by Southwest and Hawes, 19th century.
The Metropolitan Museum of Art.
Gift of I. N. Phelps Stokes, Edward S. Hawes,
Alice Mary Hawes, Marion Augusta Hawes

31

THE MOTHER COUNTRY

Benjamin Franklin

We have an old mother that peevish is grown;
She snubs us like children that scarce walk alone;
She forgets we're grown up and have sense of our own;
   Which nobody can deny, deny,
     Which nobody can deny.

If we don't obey orders, whatever the case,
She frowns, and she chides, and she loses all pati-
Ence, and sometimes she hits us a slap in the face;
   Which nobody, etc.

Her orders so odd are, we often suspect
That age has impaired her sound intellect;
But still an old mother should have due respect;
   Which nobody, etc.

Let's bear with her humors as well as we can;
But why should we bear the abuse of her man?
When servants make mischief, they earn the rattan;
   Which nobody, etc.

Know, too, ye bad neighbors, who aim to divide
The sons from the mother, that still she's our pride;
And if ye attack her, we're all of her side;
   Which nobody, etc.

We'll join in her lawsuits, to baffle all those
Who, to get what she has, will be often her foes;
For we know it must all be our own, when she goes;
   Which nobody can deny, deny,
     Which nobody can deny.

Benjamin Franklin.
Wooden figurehead by William Rush,
about 1787.
Yale University Art Gallery, New Haven

LAFAYETTE

Dolley Madison

Born, nurtured, wedded, prized, within the pale
Of peers and princes, high in camp—at court—
He hears, in joyous youth, a wild report,
Swelling the murmurs of the Western gale,
Of a young people struggling to be free!
Straight quitting all, across the wave he flies,
Aids with his sword, wealth, blood, the high emprize!
And shares the glories of its victory.
Then comes for fifty years a high romance
Of toils, reverses, sufferings, in the cause
Of man and justice, liberty and France,
Crowned, at the last, with hope and wide applause.
Champion of Freedom! Well thy race was run!
All time shall hail thee, Europe's noblest Son!

32

The Declaration of Independence by John Trumbull. 1786–97.
Oil on canvas.
Copyright Yale University Art Gallery, New Haven

Dolley Madison.
Photographic portrait by Mathew Brady,
done shortly before she died, in 1849.
Greensboro Historical Museum,
Greensboro, North Carolina

THE STAR-SPANGLED BANNER

Francis Scott Key

A New Nation

O say, can you see, by the dawn's early light,
What so proudly we hailed at the twilight's last gleaming?
Whose broad stripes and bright stars through the perilous fight,
O'er the ramparts we watched were so gallantly streaming!
And the rockets' red glare, the bombs bursting in air,
Gave proof through the night that our flag was still there.
O, say, does that star-spangled banner yet wave
O'er the land of the free, and the home of the brave?

On the shore, dimly seen through the mists of the deep,
Where the foe's haughty host in dread silence reposes,
What is that which the breeze, o'er the towering steep,
As it fitfully blows, half conceals, half discloses?
Now it catches the gleam of the morning's first beam,
In full glory reflected, now shines on the stream.
'Tis the star-spangled banner; O long may it wave
O'er the land of the free, and the home of the brave!

And where is that band who so vauntingly swore
That the havoc of war and the battle's confusion
A home and country should leave us no more?
Their blood has washed out their foul footsteps' pollution.
No refuge could save the hireling and slave
From the terror of flight, or the gloom of the grave:
And the star-spangled banner in triumph doth wave
O'er the land of the free, and the home of the brave!

Oh! thus be it ever, when freemen shall stand
Between their loved homes and the war's desolation!
Blest with victory and peace, may the heaven-rescued land
Praise the Power that hath made and preserved us a nation!
Then conquer we must, for our cause it is just,
And this be our motto: "In God is our trust."
And the star-spangled banner in triumph shall wave,
O'er the land of the free, and the home of the brave.

The flag that flew over Fort McHenry, Baltimore, Maryland,
during the attack by the British fleet in the War of 1812,
and the subject of Francis Scott Key's poem, on the opposite page.
Smithsonian Institution

AMERICA

Samuel Francis Smith

My country, 'tis of thee,
Sweet land of liberty,
   Of thee I sing;
Land where my fathers died,
Land of the pilgrims' pride,
From every mountain-side
   Let freedom ring.

My native country, thee,
Land of the noble free,
   Thy name I love;
I love thy rocks and rills,
Thy woods and templed hills;
My heart with rapture thrills
   Like that above.

Let music swell the breeze,
And ring from all the trees
   Sweet freedom's song;
Let mortal tongues awake,
Let all that breathe partake,
Let rocks their silence break.—
   The sound prolong.

Our fathers' God, to Thee,
Author of liberty,
   To Thee we sing;
Long may our land be bright
With freedom's holy light;
Protect us by Thy might,
   Great God, our King.

TRIBUTE TO AMERICA

Percy Bysshe Shelley

There is a people mighty in its youth,
   A land beyond the oceans of the west,
Where, though with rudest rites, Freedom and Truth
   Are Worshipt. From a glorious mother's breast,
   Who, since high Athens fell, among the rest
Sate like the Queen of Nations, but in woe,
   By inbred monsters outraged and opprest,
Turns to her chainless child for succor now,
It draws the milk of power in Wisdom's fullest flow.

That land is like an eagle, whose young gaze
   Feeds on the noontide beam, whose golden plume
Floats moveless on the storm, and on the blaze
   Of sunrise gleams when Earth is wrapt in gloom;
   An epitaph of glory for thy tomb
Of murdered Europe may thy fame be made,
Great People! As the sands shalt thou become;
Thy growth is swift as morn when night must fade;
The multitudinous Earth shall sleep beneath thy shade.

Yes, in the desert, there is built a home
   For Freedom! Genius is made strong to rear
The monuments of man beneath the dome
   Of a new Heaven; myriads assemble there
   Whom the proud lords of man, in rage or fear,
Drive from their wasted homes. The boon I pray
   Is this—that Cythna shall be convoyed there,—
Nay, start not at the name—America!

U.S.S. Constitution ("Old Ironsides")
entering New York harbor.
Photograph, n.d. U.S. Naval Institute, Annapolis

from
OLD IRONSIDES

Oliver Wendell Holmes

Ay, tear her tattered ensign down!
Long has it waved on high,
And many an eye has danced to see
That banner in the sky;
Beneath it rung the battle shout,
And burst the cannon's roar;—
The meteor of the ocean air
Shall sweep the clouds no more!

Her deck, once red with heroes' blood,
Where knelt the vanquished foe,
When winds were hurrying o'er the flood,
And waves were white below,
No more shall feel the victor's tread,
Or know the conquered knee;—
The harpies of the shore shall pluck
The eagle of the sea!

Oh better that her shattered hulk
Should sink beneath the wave;
Her thunders shook the mighty deep,
And there should be her grave;
Nail to the mast her holy flag,
Set every threadbare sail,
And give her to the god of storms,
The lightning and the gale!

DANCE THE BOATMAN

Anonymous

The boatman he can dance and sing
And he's the lad for any old thing.
    Dance the boatman, dance!
    Dance the boatman, dance!
He'll dance all night on his toes so light
And go down to his boat in the morning.
    Hooraw the boatman, ho!
    Spends his money with the gals ashore!
    Hooraw the boatman, ho!
    Rolling down the Ohio!

From Louisville down the Ohio,
He's known wherever them boats do go,
    Dance the boatman, dance!
    Dance the boatman, dance!
He'll drink and dance and kiss them all,
And away in his boat in the morning.
    Hooraw the boatman, ho!
    Spends his money with the girls ashore!
    Hooraw the boatman, ho!
    Rolling down the Ohio!

The girls all wait for boatman Bill,
For he's the one they all love still,
    Dance the boatman, dance!
    Dance the boatman, dance!
He'll buy them drinks and swing them high,
And leave in his boat in the morning.
    Hooraw the boatman, ho!
    Spends his money with the gals ashore!
    Hooraw the boatman, ho!
    Rolling down the Ohio!

Jolly Flatboatmen in Port *by George Caleb Bingham.*
1857. Oil on canvas. St. Louis Art Museum

from
I HEAR AMERICA SINGING

Walt Whitman

I hear America singing, the varied carols I hear,
Those of mechanics, each one singing his as it should be blithe and strong,
The carpenter singing his as he measures his plank or beam,
The mason singing his as he makes ready for work, or leaves off work,
The boatman singing what belongs to him in his boat, the deckhand singing on
    the steamboat deck,
The shoemaker singing as he sits on his bench, the hatter singing as he stands,
The wood-cutter's song, the ploughboy's on his way in the morning, or at
    noon intermission or at sundown,
The delicious singing of the mother, or of the young wife at work, or of the
    girl sewing or washing,
Each singing what belongs to him or her and to none else. . . .

Transatlantic Feelings

TO COLE, THE PAINTER,
DEPARTING FOR EUROPE

William Cullen Bryant

Thine eyes shall see the light of distant skies;
    Yet, Cole! thy heart shall bear to Europe's strand
    A living image of our own bright land,
Such as upon thy glorious canvas lies;
Lone lakes—savannas where the bison roves—
    Rocks rich with summer garlands—solemn streams—
    Skies, where the desert eagle wheels and screams—
Spring bloom and autumn blaze of boundless groves.
Fair scenes shall greet thee where thou goest—fair,
    But different—everywhere the trace of men,
Paths, homes, graves, ruins, from the lowest glen
To where life shrinks from the fierce Alpine air.
    Gaze on them, till the tears shall dim thy sight,
    But keep that earlier, wilder image bright.

Kindred Spirits by Asher B. Durand. 1849. Oil on canvas.
The painting recalls the friendship between artist Thomas Cole
and poet William Cullen Bryant—two "kindred spirits"
who celebrated the wonders of nature in America.
The New York Public Library. Astor, Lenox and Tilden Foundations

TO WHISTLER, AMERICAN

On the loan exhibit of his paintings at the Tate Gallery

Ezra Pound

You also, our first great,
Had tried all ways;
Tested and pried and worked in many fashions,
And this much gives me heart to play the game.

Here is a part that's slight, and part gone wrong,
And much of little moment, and some few
Perfect as Dürer!
"In the Studio" and these two portraits, if I had my choice!
And then these sketches in the mood of Greece?

You had your searches, your uncertainties,
And this is good to know—for us, I mean,
Who bear the brunt of our America
And try to wrench her impulse into art.

You were not always sure, not always set
To hiding night or tuning "symphonies";
Had not one style from birth, but tried and pried
And stretched and tampered with the media.

You and Abe Lincoln from that mass of dolts
Show us there's chance at least of winning through.

THE UNITED STATES

Goethe

translated by Robert Bly

America, you are luckier
Than this old continent of ours;
You have no ruined castles
And no volcanic earth.
You do not suffer
In hours of intensity
From futile memories
And pointless battles.

Concentrate on the present joyfully!
And when your children write books
May a good destiny keep them
From knight, robber, and ghost-stories.

ON AN INVITATION
TO THE UNITED STATES

Thomas Hardy

My ardours for emprize nigh lost
Since Life has bared its bones to me,
I shrink to seek a modern coast
Whose riper times have yet to be;
Where the new regions claim them free
From that long drip of human tears
Which peoples old in tragedy
Have left upon the centuried years.

For, wonning in these ancient lands,
Enchased and lettered as a tomb,
And scored with prints of perished hands,
And chronicled with dates of doom,
Though my own Being bear no bloom
I trace the lives such scenes enshrine,
Give past exemplars present room,
And their experience count as mine.

Robert Louis Stevenson *by John Singer Sargent. 1887.*
Oil on canvas.
The Taft Museum, Cincinnati.
Gift of Mr. and Mrs. Charles Phelps Taft

IN THE STATES

Robert Louis Stevenson

With half a heart I wander here
    As from an age gone by
A brother—yet though young in years,
    An elder brother, I.

You speak another tongue than mine,
    Though both were English born.
I towards the night of time decline,
    You mount into the morn.

Youth shall grow great and strong and free,
    But age must still decay:
To-morrow for the States—for me,
    England and Yesterday.

43

Westward the Course

ON RECROSSING
THE ROCKY MOUNTAINS
AFTER MANY YEARS

John Charles Frémont

Long years ago I wandered here,
In the midsummer of the year,—
 Life's summer too;
A score of horsemen here we rode,
The mountain world its glories showed,
 All fair to view.

These scenes, in glowing colors drest,
Mirrored the life within my breast,
 Its world of hopes;
The whispering woods and fragrant breeze
That stirred the grass in verdant seas
 On billowy slopes,

And glistening crag in sunlit sky,
'Mid snowy clouds piled mountains high,
 Were joys to me;
My path was o'er the prairie wide,
Or here on grander mountain side,
 To choose, all free.

The rose that waved in morning air,
And spread its dewy fragrance there,
 In careless bloom,
Gave to my heart its ruddiest hue,
O'er my glad life its color threw
 And sweet perfume.

Now changed the scene and changed the eyes,
That here once looked on glowing skies,
 Where summer smiled;
These riven trees, this wind-swept plain,
Now show the winter's dread domain,
 Its fury wild.

The Tetons and the Snake River, Grand Teton National Park, Wyoming, 1942.
Photograph by Ansel Adams.
Courtesy of the Trustees of The Ansel Adams Publishing Rights Trust, Carmel, California

The rocks rise black from storm-packed snow,
All checked the river's pleasant flow,
   Vanished the bloom;
These dreary wastes of frozen plain
Reflect my bosom's life again,
   Now lonesome gloom.

The buoyant hopes and busy life
Have ended all in hateful strife,
   And thwarted aim.
The world's rude contact killed the rose;
No more its radiant color shows
   False roads to fame.

Backward, amidst the twilight glow,
Some lingering spots yet brightly show
   On hard roads won,
Where still some grand peaks mark the way
Touched by the light of parting day
   And memory's sun.

But here thick clouds the mountains hide,
The dim horizon, bleak and wide,
   No pathway shows,
And rising gusts, and darkening sky,
Tell of the night that cometh nigh,
   The brief day's close.

WESTERN WAGONS

Rosemary and Stephen Benét

They went with axe and rifle, when the trail was still to blaze
They went with wife and children, in the prairie-schooner days
With banjo and with frying pan—Susanna, don't you cry!
For I'm off to California to get rich out there or die!

We've broken land and cleared it, but we're tired of where we are.
They say that wild Nebraska is a better place by far.
There's gold in far Wyoming, there's black earth in Ioway,
So pack up the kids and blankets, for we're moving out today.

The cowards never started and the weak died on the road,
And all across the continent the endless campfires glowed
We'd taken land and settled—but a traveler passed by—
And we're going West tomorrow—Lordy, never ask us why!

We're going West tomorrow, where the promises can't fail.
O'er the hills in legions, boys, and crowd the dusty trail!
We shall starve and freeze and suffer. We shall die, and tame the lands.
But we're going West tomorrow, with our fortune in our hands.

Camp of the Covered Wagon Train.
An on-the-spot watercolor sketch by W. C. Weisel, December 28, 1854.
Museum of Fine Arts, Boston. M. and M. Karolik Collection

PIONEER WOMAN   *Vesta Pierce Crawford*

Beneath these alien stars
   In darkness I have stood alone,
Barriers more than mountains
   Between me and my home.

And I have seen the shadows fall
   Grim patterned on the floor,
As onward passed the faces
   Beyond the cabin door.

The desert wind has waved my hair;
   Desert sands have etched my face,
And the courage of the mountains
   Has bound me to this place.

And something of its peace I've won,
   Triumphant now my day is done.
Oh, I have stood with only God
   Between me and the sun.

47

THE HIGH-LOPING COWBOY

Curley W. Fletcher

I been ridin' fer cattle the most of my life.
I ain't got no family, I ain't got no wife,
I ain't got no kith, I ain't got no kin,
I allus will finish what ere I begin.
I rode down in Texas where the cowboys are tall,
The State's pretty big but the hosses er small.
Fer singin' to cattle, I'm hard to outdo;
I'm a high-lopin' cowboy, an' a wild buckeroo.

I rode in Montana an' in Idaho;
I rode for Terasus in old Mexico.
I rope mountain lion an' grizzly bear,
I use cholla cactus fer combin' my hair.
I cross the dry desert, no water between,
I rode through Death Valley without no canteen.
At ridin' dry deserts I'm hard to outdo;
I'm a high-lopin' cowboy an' a wild buckeroo.

Why, I kin talk Spanish and Injun to boot,
I pack me a knife and a pistol to shoot.
I got no Senorita, an' I got no squaw,
I got no sweetheart, ner mother-in-law.
I never been tied to no apron strings,
I ain't no devil, but I got no wings.
At uh dodgin' the ladies, I'm hard to outdo;
I'm a high-lopin' cowboy, an' a wild buckeroo.

I drink red whiskey, an' I don't like beer,
I don't like mutton, but I do like steer.
I will let you alone if you leave me be,
But don't you get tough an' crawl on me.
I'll fight you now at the drop of a hat,
You'll think you're sacked up with a scratchin' wild cat.
At rough ready mixin' I'm hard to outdo;
I'm a high-lopin' cowboy, an' a wild buckeroo.

SPANISH JOHNNY

Willa Cather

The old West, the old time,
    The old wind singing through
The red, red grass a thousand miles,
    And, Spanish Johnny, you!
He'd sit beside the water-ditch
    When all his herd was in,
And never mind a child, but sing
    To his mandolin.

The big stars, the blue night,
    The moon-enchanted plain:
The olive man who never spoke,
    But sang the songs of Spain.
His speech with men was wicked talk—
    To hear it was a sin;
But those were golden things he said
    To his mandolin.

The gold songs, the gold stars,
    The world so golden then:
And the hand so tender to a child
    Had killed so many men.
He died a hard death long ago
    Before the Road came in;
The night before he swung, he sang
    To his mandolin.

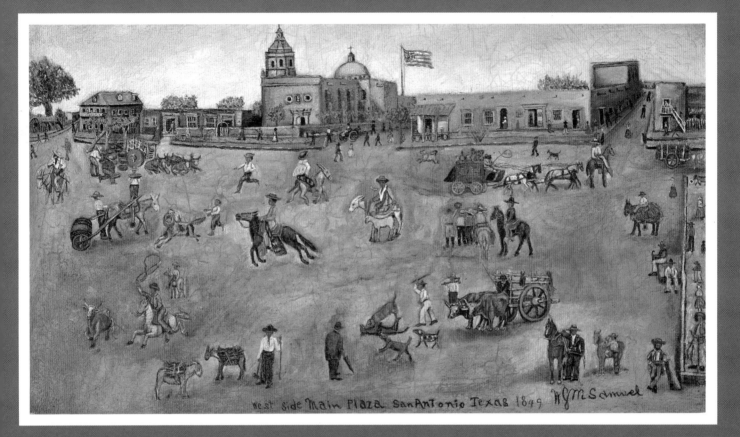

West Side Main Plaza by William M. G. Samuel. 1849. Oil.
Courtesy San Antonio Museum Association, San Antonio, Texas

HE DONE HIS LEVEL BEST

Mark Twain

Was he a mining on the flat—
   He done it with a zest;
Was he a leading of the choir—
   He done his level best.

If he'd a reg'lar task to do,
   He never took no rest;
Or if 'twas off-and-on—the same—
   He done his level best.

If he was preachin' on his beat,
   He'd tramp from east to west,
And north to south—in cold and heat
   He done his level best.

He'd yank a sinner outen (Hades),*
   And land him with the blest;
Then snatch a prayer 'n waltz in again,
   And do his level best.

He'd cuss and sing and howl and pray,
   And dance and drink and jest,
And lie and steal—all one to him—
   He done his level best.

Whate'er this man was sot to do,
   He done it with a zest;
No matter *what* his contract was,
   HE'D DO HIS LEVEL BEST.

* Here I have taken a slight liberty with the original MS. "Hades" does not make such good metre as the other word of one syllable, but it sounds better. (Mark Twain's note. Supposedly the verse was written by Simon Wheeler, narrator of the Jumping Frog tale.)

Texas Ranger. Photograph, n.d.
Emory Cantey Collection, Aurora, Colorado

THE TEXAS RANGER   *Margie B. Boswell*

In the old, old days when the West was young,
The Ranger rode the trail.
The thunder of hoof-beats was his song,
And the Right his Holy Grail.

He was tall and straight as Indian corn;
Weathered and brown as a berry.
His draw was as quick as the redstart's flight;
He was Law on the Texas prairie.

The sky was his roof; the earth his bed;
His saddle a ready pillow.
His friends were the quail, the wild curlew
And the shade of the button willow.

You say the Ranger rides no more?
Listen, some night, if you will
When the wind is soft as a bluebird's call,
And the prairies are dark and still,

And you may hear the pound of hoofs,
You may catch the fleeting shadow
Of a horse and rider charging across
The grassy moonlit meadow.

Through windy darkness and brittle dawn,
He follows his mighty quest,
For the trail he cut so long ago
Runs straight through the heart of the West.

51

CHICAGO

Bret Harte

Blackened and bleeding, helpless, panting, prone,
On the charred fragments of her shattered throne
Lies she who stood but yesterday alone.
Queen of the West! by some enchanter taught
To lift the glory of Aladdin's court,
Then lose the spell that all that wonder wrought.

Like her own prairies by some chance seed sown,
Like her own prairies in one brief day grown,
Like her own prairies in one fierce night mown.

She lifts her voice, and in her pleading call
We hear the cry of Macedon to Paul,
The cry for help that makes her kin to all.

But haply with wan fingers may she feel
The silver cup hid in the proffered meal,
The gifts her kinship and our loves reveal.

The Great Fire at Chicago, October 8, 1871.
Lithograph by Currier & Ives.
Museum of the City of New York

AN ARMY CORPS ON THE MARCH

Walt Whitman

With its cloud of skirmishers in advance,
With now the sound of a single shot snapping like a whip, and now
   an irregular volley,
The swarming ranks press on and on, the dense brigades press on,
Glittering dimly, toiling under the sun—the dust-cover'd men,
In columns rise and fall to the undulations of the ground,
With artillery interspers'd—the wheels rumble, the horses sweat,
As the army corps advances.

CAVALRY CROSSING A FORD

Walt Whitman

A line in long array where they wind betwixt green islands,
They take a serpentine course, their arms flash in the sun—hark to
   the musical clank,
Behold the silvery river, in it the splashing horses loitering stop to drink,
Behold the brown-faced men, each group, each person a picture, the negligent
   rest on the saddles,
Some emerge on the opposite bank, others are just entering the ford—while,
Scarlet and blue and snowy white,
The guidon flags flutter gayly in the wind.

BIVOUAC ON A MOUNTAIN SIDE

Walt Whitman

I see before me now a traveling army halting,
Below a fertile valley spread, with barns and the orchards of summer,
Behind, the terraced sides of a mountain, abrupt, in places rising high,
Broken, with rocks, with clinging cedars, with tall shapes dingily seen,
The numerous camp-fires scatter'd near and far, some away up on the mountain,
The shadowy forms of men and horses, looming, large-sized, flickering,
And over all the sky—the sky! far, far out of reach, studded, breaking out,
   the eternal stars.

Home Sweet Home by Winslow Homer.
1863. Oil on canvas.
Private collection.
Courtesy Hirschl and Adler Galleries, New York

COMMEMORATIVE OF A
NAVAL VICTORY

Herman Melville

Sailors there are of gentlest breed,
    Yet strong, like every goodly thing;
The discipline of arms refines,
    And the wave gives tempering.
    The damasked blade its beam can fling;
It lends the last grave grace:
The hawk, the hound, and sworded nobleman
    In Titian's picture for a king,
Are of hunter or warrior race.

In social halls a favored guest
    In years that follow victory won,
How sweet to feel your festal fame
    In woman's glance instinctive thrown:
    Repose is yours—your deed is known,
It musks the amber wine;
It lives, and sheds a light from storied days
    Rich as October sunsets brown,
Which make the barren place to shine.

But seldom the laurel wreath is seen
    Unmixed with pensive pansies dark;
There's a light and a shadow on every man
    Who at last attains his lifted mark—
    Nursing through night the ethereal spark.
Elate he never can be;
He feels that spirit which glad had hailed his worth,
    Sleep in oblivion.—The shark
Glides white through the phosphorus sea.

The Alabama and Kearsage by Edouard Manet.
1864. Oil on canvas.
The painting records a battle during the Civil War,
June 19, 1864, off the French coast;
the Alabama was Confederate and the Kearsage was Union.
Philadelphia Museum of Art. The John G. Johnson Collection

from

BARBARA FRIETCHIE

John Greenleaf Whittier

Up from the meadows rich with corn,
Clear in the cool September morn,
The clustered spires of Frederick stand
Green-walled by the hills of Maryland.

Round about them orchards sweep,
Apple and peach tree fruited deep,
Fair as the garden of the Lord
To the eyes of the famished rebel horde,

On that pleasant morn of the early fall
When Lee marched over the mountain-wall;
Over the mountains winding down,
Horse and foot, into Frederick town.

Forty flags with their silver stars,
Forty flags with their crimson bars,
Flapped in the morning wind: the sun
Of noon looked down, and saw not one.

Up rose old Barbara Frietchie then,
Bowed with her fourscore years and ten;
Bravest of all in Frederick town,
She took up the flag the men hauled down,

In her attic window the staff she set,
To show that one heart was loyal yet.
Up the street came the rebel tread,
Stonewall Jackson riding ahead.

Under his slouched hat left and right
He glanced; the old flag met his sight.
"Halt!"—the dust-brown ranks stood fast.
"Fire!"—out blazed the rifle-blast.

It shivered the window, pane and sash;
It rent the banner with seam and gash.
Quick, as it fell, from the broken staff
Dame Barbara snatched the silken scarf.

She leaned far out on the window-sill,
And shook it forth with a royal will.
"Shoot, if you must, this old gray head,
But spare your country's flag," she said.

A shade of sadness, a blush of shame,
Over the face of the leader came;
The nobler nature within him stirred
To life at that woman's deed and word;

"Who touches a hair of yon gray head
Dies like a dog! March on!" he said.
All day long through Frederick street
Sounded the tread of marching feet:

All day long that free flag tost
Over the heads of the rebel host.
Ever its torn folds rose and fell
On the loyal winds that loved it well;

And through the hill-gaps sunset light
Shone over it with a warm good-night.
Barbara Frietchie's work is o'er,
And the Rebel rides on his raids no more.

Honor to her! and let a tear
Fall, for her sake, on Stonewall's bier.
Over Barbara Frietchie's grave,
Flag of Freedom and Union, wave!

Peace and order and beauty draw
Round thy symbol of light and law;
And ever the stars above look down
On thy stars below in Frederick town!

American Fantasy. About 1860.
Cut paper with embossed details and watercolor.
Copyright © 1987 Sotheby's, Inc., New York

WAR IS KIND *Stephen Crane*

Do not weep, maiden, for war is kind.
Because your lover threw wild hands toward the sky
Do not weep.
War is kind.

Hoarse, booming drums of the regiment,
Little souls who thirst for fight,
These men were born to drill and die.
The unexplained glory flies above them,
Great is the battle-god, great, and his kingdom—
A field where a thousand corpses lie.

Do not weep, babe, for war is kind.
Because your father tumbled in the yellow trenches,
Raged at his breast, gulped and died,

Do not weep.
War is kind.

Swift blazing flag of the regiment,
Eagle with crest of red and gold,
These men were born to drill and die.
Point for them the virtue of slaughter,
Make plain to them the excellence of killing
And a field where a thousand corpses lie.

Mother whose heart hung humble as a button
On the bright splendid shroud of your son,
Do not weep.
War is kind.

O CAPTAIN! MY CAPTAIN!

Walt Whitman

O Captain! my Captain! our fearful trip is done;
The ship has weather'd every rack, the prize we sought is won;
The port is near, the bells I hear, the people all exulting,
While follow eyes the steady keel, the vessel grim and daring:
        But O heart! heart! heart!
          O the bleeding drops of red,
             Where on the deck my Captain lies,
               Fallen cold and dead.

            O Captain! my Captain! rise up and hear the bells;
            Rise up—for you the flag is flung—for you the bugle trills;
            For you bouquets and ribbon'd wreaths—for you the shores a-crowding;
            For you they call, the swaying mass, their eager faces turning;
                Here Captain! dear father!
                  This arm beneath your head;
                    It is some dream that on the deck,
                      You've fallen cold and dead.

A Harvest of death.
Photograph by Alexander Gardner and Timothy O'Sullivan, 1863.
The New York Public Library. Rare Books & Manuscripts Division

Abraham Lincoln.
Photograph by Alexander Gardner, April 10, 1865.
Considered the last photograph taken of Lincoln.
National Portrait Gallery, Smithsonian Institution

My Captain does not answer, his lips are pale and still;
My father does not feel my arm, he has no pulse nor will;
The ship is anchor'd safe and sound, its voyage closed and done;
From fearful trip, the victor ship, comes in with object won;
Exult, O shores, and ring, O bells!
But I, with mournful tread,
Walk the deck my Captain lies,
Fallen cold and dead.

ODE TO THE CONFEDERATE DEAD   *Allen Tate*

Row after row with strict impunity
The headstones yield their names to the element,
The wind whirrs without recollection;
In the riven troughs the splayed leaves
Pile up, of nature the casual sacrament
To the seasonal eternity of death;
Then driven by the fierce scrutiny
Of heaven to their election in the vast breath,
They sough the rumour of mortality.

Autumn is desolation in the plot
Of a thousand acres where these memories grow
From the inexhaustible bodies that are not
Dead, but feed the grass row after rich row.
Think of the autumns that have come and gone!—
Ambitious November with the humors of the year,
With a particular zeal for every slab,
Staining the uncomfortable angels that rot
On the slabs, a wing chipped here, an arm there:
The brute curiosity of an angel's stare
Turns you, like them, to stone,
Transforms the heaving air
Till plunged to a heavier world below
You shift your sea-space blindly
Heaving, turning like the blind crab.

> Dazed by the wind, only the wind
> The leaves flying, plunge

You know who have waited by the wall
The twilight certainty of an animal,
Those midnight restitutions of the blood
You know—the immitigable pines, the smoky frieze
Of the sky, the sudden call: you know the rage,
The cold pool left by the mounting flood,
Of muted Zeno and Parmenides.
You who have waited for the angry resolution
Of those desires that should be yours tomorrow,
You know the unimportant shrift of death
And praise the vision
And praise the arrogant circumstance
Of those who fall

Rank upon rank, hurried beyond decision—
Here by the sagging gate, stopped by the wall.

> Seeing, seeing only the leaves
> Flying, plunge and expire

Turn your eyes to the immoderate past,
Turn to the inscrutable infantry rising
Demons out of the earth—they will not last.
Stonewall, Stonewall, and the sunken fields of hemp,
Shiloh, Antietam, Malvern Hill, Bull Run.
Lost in that orient of the thick-and-fast
You will curse the setting sun.

> Cursing only the leaves crying
> Like an old man in a storm

You hear the shout, the crazy hemlocks point
With troubled fingers to the silence which
Smothers you, a mummy, in time.

> The hound bitch
> Toothless and dying, in a musty cellar
> Hears the wind only.

> Now that the salt of their blood
Stiffens the saltier oblivion of the sea,
Seals the malignant purity of the flood,
What shall we who count our days and bow
Our heads with a commemorial woe
In the ribboned coats of grim felicity,
What shall we say of the bones, unclean,
Whose verdurous anonymity will grow?
The ragged arms, the ragged heads and eyes
Lost in these acres of the insane green?
The gray lean spiders come, they come and go;
In a tangle of willows without light
The singular screech-owl's tight
Invisible lyric seeds the mind
With the furious murmur of their chivalry.

> We shall say only the leaves
> Flying, plunge and expire

Last Civil War Veteran by Larry Rivers.
1961. Oil on canvas.
Mr. and Mrs. David Anderson, New York
(Photograph by Richard P. Meyer)

We shall say only the leaves whispering
In the improbable mist of nightfall
That flies on multiple wing;
Night is the beginning and the end
And in between the ends of distraction
Waits mute speculation, the patient curse
That stones the eyes, or like the jaguar leaps
For his own image in a jungle pool, his victim.
What shall we say who have knowledge

Carried to the heart? Shall we take the act
To the grave? Shall we, more hopeful, set up the grave
In the house? The ravenous grave?

                                    Leave now
The shut gate and the decomposing wall:
The gentle serpent, green in the mulberry bush,
Riots with his tongue through the hush—
Sentinel of the grave who counts us all!

63

Man and Nature

NATURE

Henry David Thoreau

O Nature! I do not aspire
To be the highest in thy quire,—
To be a meteor in the sky,
Or comet that may range on high;
Only a zephyr that may blow
Among the reeds by the river low;
Give me thy most privy place
Where to run my airy race.

In some withdrawn, unpublic mead
Let me sigh upon a reed,
Or in the woods, with leafy din,
Whisper the still evening in:
Some still work give me to do,—
Only—be it near to you!

For I'd rather be thy child
And pupil, in the forest wild,
Than be the king of men elsewhere,
And most sovereign slave of care:
To have one moment of thy dawn,
Than share the city's year forlorn.

The Peaceable Kingdom. *Edward Hicks. About 1840–45. Oil on canvas.*
The Brooklyn Museum. Dick S. Ramsay Fund

THE DARK HILLS

Edwin Arlington Robinson

Dark hills at evening in the west,
Where sunset hovers like a sound
Of golden horns that sang to rest
Old bones of warriors under ground,
Far now from all the bannered ways
Where flash the legions of the sun,
You fade—as if the last of days
Were fading, and all wars were done.

WRITTEN IN AUTUMN

Thomas Cole

Another year like a frail flower is bound
In time's sere withering aye to cling,
Eternity, thy shadowy temples round,
Like to the musick of a broken string
That ne'er can sound again, 'tis past and gone,
Its dying sweetness dwells within memory alone—

Year after year with silent lapse fleet by;
Each seems more brief than that which went before;
The weeks of youth are years; but manhood's fly
On swifter wings, years seem but weeks, no more—
So glides a river through a thirsty land,
Wastes as it flows till lost amid the Desert sand.

The green of Spring which melts the heart like love
Is faded long ago, the fiercer light
Of hues autumnal, fire the quivering grove,
And rainbow tints array the mountain-height—
A pomp there is, a glory on the hills
And gold and crimson stream reflected from the rills.

But 'tis a dying pomp a gorgeous shroud
T' enwrap the lifeless year—I scarce forgive
The seeming mockery of death; but that aloud
A voice sounds through my soul—"All things live
To die and die to be renewed again,
Therefore we should rejoice at death and not complain."

View on the Catskill, Early Autumn by Thomas Cole.
1837. Oil on canvas.
The Metropolitan Museum of Art.
Gift in memory of Jonathan Sturges
by his children, 1895

NIGHT ON THE PRAIRIES

Walt Whitman

Night on the prairies,
The supper is over, the fire on the ground burns low,
The wearied emigrants sleep, wrapt in their blankets;
I walk by myself—I stand and look at the stars, which I think now
       I never realized before.

Now I absorb immortality and peace,
I admire death and test propositions.

How plenteous! how spiritual! how resumé!
The same old man and soul—the same old aspirations, and the same content.

I was thinking the day most splendid till I saw what the not-day exhibited,
I was thinking this globe enough till there sprang out so noiseless around me
       myriads of other globes.

Now while the great thoughts of space and eternity fill me I will measure
        myself by them,
And now touch'd with the lives of other globes arrived as far along as those
       of the earth,
Or waiting to arrive, or pass'd on farther than those of the earth,
I henceforth no more ignore them than I ignore my own life,
Or the lives of the earth arrived as far as mine, or waiting to arrive.

O I see now that life cannot exhibit all to me, as the day cannot,
I see that I am to wait for what will be exhibited by death.

Walt Whitman.
Photograph by Thomas Eakins, about 1888.
In his Preface to Leaves of Grass, *1855, Whitman wrote:*
"The United States themselves are essentially the greatest poem."
The Philadelphia Museum of Art.
Bequest of Mark Lutz

I SAW IN LOUISIANA
A LIVE-OAK GROWING

Walt Whitman

I saw in Louisiana a live-oak growing,
All alone stood it and the moss hung down from the branches,
Without any companion it grew there uttering joyous leaves of dark green
And its look, rude, unbending, lusty, made me think of myself,
But I wonder'd how it could utter joyous leaves standing alone there without
        its friend near, for I knew I could not,
And I broke off a twig with a certain number of leaves upon it, and
        twined around it a little moss,
And brought it away, and I have placed it in sight in my room,
It is not needed to remind me as of my own dear friends,
(For I believe lately I think of little else than of them,)
Yet it remains to me a curious token, it makes me think of manly love;
For all that, and though the live-oak glistens there in Louisiana solitary in a
        wide flat space,
Uttering joyous leaves all its life without a friend a lover near,
I know very well I could not.

from
SMOKE AND STEEL

Carl Sandburg

   A bar of steel—it is only
Smoke at the heart of it, smoke and the blood of a man.
A runner of fire ran in it, ran out, ran somewhere else,
And left—smoke and the blood of a man
And the finished steel, chilled and blue.
So fire runs in, runs out, runs somewhere else again,
And the bar of steel is a gun, a wheel, a nail, a shovel,
A rudder under the sea, a steering-gear in the sky;
And always dark in the heart and through it,
    Smoke and the blood of a man.
Pittsburgh, Youngstown, Gary—they make their steel with men.

Ironworkers—Noontime *by Thomas P. Anshutz.*
About 1881. Oil on canvas.
The Fine Arts Museums of San Francisco.
Gift of Mr. and Mrs. John D. Rockefeller 3rd

THE VILLAGE BLACKSMITH

Henry Wadsworth Longfellow

Under a spreading chestnut-tree
   The village smithy stands;
The smith, a mighty man is he,
   With large and sinewy hands;
And the muscles of his brawny arms
   Are strong as iron bands.

His hair is crisp, and black, and long,
   His face is like the tan;
His brow is wet with honest sweat,
   He earns whate'er he can,
And looks the whole world in the face,
   For he owes not any man.

Week in, week out, from morn till night,
   You can hear his bellows blow;
You can hear him swing his heavy sledge,
   With measured beat and slow,
Like a sexton ringing the village bell,
   When the evening sun is low.

And children coming home from school
   Look in at the open door;
They love to see the flaming forge,
   And hear the bellows roar,
And catch the burning sparks that fly
   Like chaff from a threshing-floor.

He goes on Sunday to the church,
   And sits among his boys;
He hears the parson pray and preach,
   He hears his daughter's voice,
Singing in the village choir,
   And it makes his heart rejoice.

It sounds to him like her mother's voice,
   Singing in Paradise!
He needs must think of her once more,
   How in the grave she lies;
And with his hard, rough hand he wipes
   A tear out of his eyes.

Toiling,—rejoicing,—sorrowing,
   Onward through life he goes;
Each morning sees some task begin,
   Each evening sees it close;
Something attempted, something done,
   Has earned a night's repose.

Thanks, thanks to thee, my worthy friend,
   For the lesson thou hast taught!
Thus at the flaming forge of life
   Our fortunes must be wrought;
Thus on its sounding anvil shaped
   Each burning deed and thought.

The Village Blacksmith.
Lithograph by Currier & Ives, 1864.
The Museum of the City of New York. The Harry T. Peters Collection

from
THE BAREFOOT BOY

John Greenleaf Whittier

Oh for boyhood's painless play,
Sleep that wakes in laughing day,
Health that mocks the doctor's rules,
Knowledge never learned of schools,
Of the wild bee's morning chase,
Of the wild-flower's time and place,
Flight of fowl and habitude
Of the tenants of the wood;
How the tortoise bears his shell,
How the woodchuck digs his cell,
And the ground-mole sinks his well;
How the robin feeds her young,
How the oriole's nest is hung;
Where the whitest lilies blow,
Where the freshest berries grow,
Where the ground-nut trails its vine,
Where the wood-grape's clusters shine;
Of the black wasp's cunning way,
Mason of his walls of clay,
And the architectural plans
Of gray hornet artisans!
For, eschewing books and tasks,
Nature answers all he asks;
Hand in hand with her he walks,
Face to face with her he talks,
Part and parcel of her joy,—
Blessings on the barefoot boy!

Two of Eakins' nephews at the farm in Avondale, Pennsylvania.
Photograph by Thomas Eakins, about 1883–90.
The J. Paul Getty Museum, Malibu, California

from
JOHN BROWN'S BODY

Stephen Vincent Benét

He was a farmer, he didn't think much of towns,
The wheels, the vastness.
He liked the wide fields, the yellows, the lonely browns,
The black ewe's fastness.

Out of his body grows revolving steel,
Out of his body grows the spinning wheel
Made up of wheels, the new, mechanic birth,
No longer bound by toil
To the unsparing soil
Or the old furrow-line,
The great, metallic beast
Expanding West and East,
His heart a spinning coil,
His juices burning oil,
His body serpentine.

John Brown Going to His Hanging by Horace Pippin.
1942. Oil on canvas.
The Pennsylvania Academy of the Fine Arts, Philadelphia.
John Lambert Fund

from
SNOW-BOUND

John Greenleaf Whittier

The sun that brief December day
Rose cheerless over hills of gray,
And, darkly circled, gave at noon
A sadder light than waning moon.
Slow tracing down the thickening sky
Its mute and ominous prophecy,
A portent seeming less than threat,
It sank from sight before it set.
A chill no coat, however stout,
Of homespun stuff could quite shut out,
A hard, dull bitterness of cold,
That checked, mid-vein, the circling race
Of life-blood in the sharpened face,
The coming of the snow-storm told.
The wind blew east; we heard the roar
Of Ocean on his wintry shore,
And felt the strong pulse throbbing there
Beat with low rhythm our inland air.

Unwarmed by any sunset light
The gray day darkened into night,
A night made hoary with the swarm,
And whirl-dance of the blinding storm,
As zigzag, wavering to and fro,
Crossed and recrossed the wingèd snow:
And ere the early bedtime came
The white drift piled the window-frame,
And through the glass the clothes-line posts
Looked in like tall and sheeted ghosts.

A VISIT FROM ST. NICHOLAS

Clement Moore

'Twas the night before Christmas, when all through the house
Not a creature was stirring, not even a mouse.
The stockings were hung by the chimney with care,
In hopes that St. Nicholas soon would be there;
The children were nestled all snug in their beds,
While visions of sugar-plums danced in their heads;
And mamma in her 'kerchief, and I in my cap,
Had just settled our brains for a long winter's nap,
When out on the lawn there arose such a clatter,
I sprang from the bed to see what was the matter.
Away to the window I flew like a flash,
Tore open the shutters and threw up the sash.
The moon on the breast of the new-fallen snow
Gave the luster of mid-day to objects below,
When, what to my wondering eyes should appear,
But a miniature sleigh, and eight tiny reindeer,
With a little old driver, so lively and quick,
I knew in a moment it must be St. Nick.
More rapid than eagles his coursers they came,
And he whistled, and shouted, and called them by name:
"Now, *Dasher!* now, *Dancer!* now, *Prancer* and *Vixen!*
On, *Comet!* on, *Cupid!* on, *Donder* and *Blitzen!*
To the top of the porch! to the top of the wall!
Now dash away! dash away! dash away all!"
As dry leaves that before the wild hurricane fly,
When they meet with an obstacle, mount to the sky,
So up to the house-top the coursers they flew,
With the sleigh full of toys, and St. Nicholas too.
And then, in a twinkling, I heard on the roof
The prancing and pawing of each little hoof.
As I drew in my head, and was turning around,
Down the chimney St. Nicholas came with a bound.
He was dressed all in fur, from his head to his foot,
And his clothes were all tarnished with ashes and soot;
A bundle of toys he had flung on his back,
And he looked like a peddler just opening his pack.
His eyes—how they twinkled! his dimples how merry!
His cheeks were like roses, his nose like a cherry!
His droll little mouth was drawn up like a bow,
And the beard of his chin was as white as the snow;

The Christmas Tree,
1890 by *Julian Alden Weir.*
Oil on canvas.
Private collection

The stump of a pipe he held tight in his teeth,
And the smoke it encircled his head like a wreath;
He had a broad face and a little round belly,
That shook, when he laughed, like a bowlful of jelly.
He was chubby and plump, a right jolly old elf,
And I laughed when I saw him, in spite of myself;
A wink of his eye and a twist of his head,
Soon gave me to know I had nothing to dread.
He spoke not a word, but went straight to his work,
And filled all the stockings; then turned with a jerk,
And laying his finger aside of his nose
And giving a nod, up the chimney he rose.
He sprang to his sleigh, to his team gave a whistle,
And away they all flew like the down of a thistle,
But I heard him exclaim, ere he drove out of sight,
"Happy Christmas to all, and to all a good-night."

79

CASEY AT THE BAT

E. L. *Thayer*

The outlook wasn't brilliant for the Mudville nine that day;
The score stood four to two with but one inning more to play.
And then when Cooney died at first, and Barrows did the same,
A sickly silence fell upon the patrons of the game.

A straggling few got up to go in deep despair. The rest
Clung to that hope which springs eternal in the human breast;
They thought if only Casey could but get a whack at that—
We'd put up even money now with Casey at the bat.

But Flynn preceded Casey, as did also Johnnie Blake,
And the former was a lulu and the latter was a cake;
So upon that stricken multitude grim melancholy sat,
For there seemed but little chance of Casey's getting to the bat.

But Flynn let drive a single, to the wonderment of all,
And Blake, the much despisèd, tore the cover off the ball;
And when the dust had lifted, and the men saw what had occurred,
There was Johnnie safe at second and Flynn a-hugging third.

Then from 5,000 throats and more there rose a lusty yell;
It rumbled through the valley, it rattled in the dell;
It knocked upon the mountain and recoiled upon the flat,
For Casey, mighty Casey, was advancing to the bat.

There was ease in Casey's manner as he stepped into his place;
There was pride in Casey's bearing and a smile on Casey's face.
And when, responding to the cheers, he lightly doffed his hat,
No stranger in the crowd could doubt 'twas Casey at the bat.

Ten thousand eyes were on him as he rubbed his hands with dirt;
Five thousand tongues applauded when he wiped them on his shirt.
Then while the writhing pitcher ground the ball into his hip,
Defiance gleamed in Casey's eye, a sneer curled Casey's lip.

And now the leather-covered sphere came hurtling through the air,
And Casey stood a-watching it in haughty grandeur there.
Close by the sturdy batsman the ball unheeded sped—
"That ain't my style," said Casey. "Strike one," the umpire said.

From the benches, black with people, there went up a muffled roar,
Like the beating of the storm-waves on a stern and distant shore.
"Kill him! Kill the umpire!" shouted some one on the stand;
And it's likely they'd have killed him had not Casey raised his hand.

With a smile of Christian charity great Casey's visage shone;
He stilled the rising tumult; he bade the game go on;
He signaled to the pitcher, and once more the spheroid flew;
But Casey still ignored it, and the umpire said, "Strike two."

"Fraud!" cried the maddened thousands, and echo answered fraud;
But one scornful look from Casey and the audience was awed.
They saw his face grow stern and cold, they saw his muscles strain,
And they knew that Casey wouldn't let that ball go by again.

The sneer is gone from Casey's lip, his teeth are clenched in hate;
He pounds with cruel violence his bat upon the plate.
And now the pitcher holds the ball, and now he lets it go,
And now the air is shattered by the force of Casey's blow.

Oh, somewhere in this favored land the sun is shining bright;
The band is playing somewhere, and somewhere hearts are light,
And somewhere men are laughing, and somewhere children shout;
But there is no joy in Mudville—mighty Casey has struck out.

ANNABEL LEE

Edgar Allan Poe

It was many and many a year ago,
    In a kingdom by the sea,
That a maiden there lived whom you may know
    By the name of Annabel Lee;
And this maiden she lived with no other thought
    Than to love and be loved by me.

I was a child and *she* was a child,
    In this kingdom by the sea:
But we loved with a love that was more than love—
    I and my Annabel Lee;
With a love that the winged seraphs of heaven
    Coveted her and me.

And this was the reason that, long ago,
    In this kingdom by the sea,
A wind blew out of a cloud, chilling
    My beautiful Annabel Lee;
So that her high-born kinsman came
    And bore her away from me,
To shut her up in a sepulchre
    In this kingdom by the sea.

The angels, not half so happy in heaven,
    Went envying her and me—
Yes!—that was the reason (as all men know,
    In this kingdom by the sea)
That the wind came out of the cloud by night,
    Chilling and killing my Annabel Lee.

But our love it was stronger by far than the love
    Of those who were older than we—
    Of many far wiser than we—
And neither the angels in heaven above,
    Nor the demons down under the sea,
Can ever dissever my soul from the soul
    Of the beautiful Annabel Lee,

For the moon never beams, without bringing me dreams
    Of the beautiful Annabel Lee;
And the stars never rise, but I feel the bright eyes
    Of the beautiful Annabel Lee;
And so, all the night-tide, I lie down by the side
Of my darling—my darling—my life and my bride,
    In the sepulchre there by the sea,
    In her tomb by the sounding sea.

Annabel Lee
by James McNeill Whistler.
About 1870.
Crayon and pastel
on brown paper.
Freer Gallery of Art,
Smithsonian Institution

Opening Doors

THREE THINGS ENCHANTED HIM

Anna Akhmatova
translated by Stanley Kunitz with Max Hayward

Three things enchanted him:
white peacocks, evensong,
and faded maps of America.
He couldn't stand bawling brats,
or raspberry jam with his tea,
or womanish hysteria.
. . . And he was tied to me.

THE NETWORK

Arthur Sze

In 1861, George Hew sailed in a rowboat
from the Pearl river, China, across
the Pacific ocean to San Francisco.
He sailed alone. The photograph of him
in a museum disappeared. But, in the mind,
he is intense, vivid, alive. What is
this fact but another fact in a world
of facts, another truth in a vast network
of truths? It is a red maple leaf
flaming out at the end of its life,
revealing an incredibly rich and complex
network of branching veins. We live
in such a network: the world is opaque,
translucent, or, suddenly, lucid,
vibrant. The air is alive and hums
then. Speech is too slow to the mind.
And the mind's speech is so quick it breaks
the sound barrier and shatters glass.

THE NEW COLOSSUS

Emma Lazarus

Not like the brazen giant of Greek fame,
With conquering limbs astride from land to land;
Here at our sea-washed, sunset gates shall stand
A mighty woman with a torch, whose flame
Is the imprisoned lightning, and her name
Mother of Exiles. From her beacon-hand
Glows world-wide welcome; her mild eyes command
The air-bridged harbor that twin cities frame.
"Keep, ancient lands, your storied pomp!" cries she
With silent lips. "Give me your tired, your poor,
Your huddled masses yearning to breathe free,
The wretched refuse of your teeming shore.
Send these, the homeless, tempest-tost to me,
I lift my lamp beside the golden door!"

84

Unveiling of the Statue of Liberty.
Quilt by Katherine Westphal, 1964.
Fabric batiked, quilted, and embroidered.
National Museum of American Art, Renwick Gallery,
Smithsonian Institution. Gift of the artist

TO INEZ MILHOLLAND

Edna St. Vincent Millay

(Read in Washington, November eighteenth, 1923,
at the unveiling of a statue of three leaders in the
cause of Equal Rights for Women)

Upon this marble bust that is not I
Lay the round, formal wreath that is not fame;
But in the forum of my silenced cry
Root ye the living tree whose sap is flame.
I, that was proud and valiant, am no more;—
Save as a dream that wanders wide and late,
Save as a wind that rattles the stout door,
Troubling the ashes in the sheltered grate.
The stone will perish; I shall be twice dust.
Only my standard on a taken hill
Can cheat the mildew and the red-brown rust
And make immortal my adventurous will.
Even now the silk is tugging at the staff:
Take up the song; forget the epitaph.

Edna St. Vincent Millay.
Photograph, about 1912.
Library of Congress

PROSPECTIVE IMMIGRANTS
PLEASE NOTE

Adrienne Rich

Either you will
go through this door
or you will not go through.

If you go through
there is always the risk
of remembering your name.

Things look at you doubly
and you must look back
and let them happen.

If you do not go through
it is possible
to live worthily

to maintain your attitudes
to hold your position
to die bravely

but much will blind you,
much will evade you,
at what cost who knows?

The door itself
makes no promises.
It is only a door.

Immigrants at Ellis Island, New York.
Photograph, about 1912.
Library of Congress

World War I

CAMOUFLAGED TROOP-SHIP
Boston Harbour   *Amy Lowell*

Uprightness,
Masts, one behind another,
Syncopated beyond and between one another,
Clouding together,
Becoming confused.
A mist of grey, blurring stems
Platformed upon horizontal thicknesses.
Decks,
Bows and sterns escaping fore and aft,
A long line of flatness
Darker than the fog of masts,
More solid,
Monotonous grey.
Dull smokestacks
Plotting lustreless clouds.
An ebb-tide
Slowly sucking the refuse of a harbour
Seaward.

The ferry turns;
And there,
On the starboard quarter,
Thrust out from the vapour-wall of ships:
Colour.
Against the perpendicular:
Obliqueness.
In front of the horizontal:
A crenelated edge.
A vessel, grooved and conical,
Shell-shaped, flower-flowing,
Gothic, bizarre, and unrelated.
Black spirals over cream-colour
Broken at a half-way point.
A slab of black amidships.
At the stern,
Lines:
Rising from the water,
Curled round and over,

Whorled, scattered,
Drawn upon one another.
Snakes starting from a still ocean,
Writhing over cream-colour,
Crashed upon and cut down
By a flat, impinging horizon.

The sea is grey and low,
But the vessel is high with upthrusting lines:
Hair lines incessantly moving,
Broad bands of black turning evenly over emptiness,
Intorting upon their circuits,
Teasing the eye with indefinite motion,
Coming from nothing,
Ending without cessation.
Drowned hair drifting against mother-of-pearl;
Kelp-aprons
Shredded upon a yellow beach;
Black spray
Salted over cream-grey wave-tops.

You hollow into rising water,
You double-turn under the dripped edges of clouds,
You move in a hundred directions,
And keep to a course the eye cannot see.
Your terrible lines
Are swift as the plunge of a kingfisher;
They vanish as one traces them,
They are constantly vanishing,
And yet you swing at anchor in the grey harbour
Waiting for your quota of troops.
Men will sail in you,
Netted in whirling paint,
Held like brittle eggs
In an osier basket.
They will sail,
Over black-skinned water,
Into a distance of cream-colour and
     vague shadow-shotted blue.

The ferry whistle blows for the landing.
Start the engine
That we may not block
The string of waiting carts.

The Navy Needs You.
World War I recruiting poster by J. M. Flagg.
West Point Museum Collections, United States Military Academy

I HAVE A RENDEZVOUS WITH DEATH

Alan Seeger

I have a rendezvous with Death
At some disputed barricade,
When Spring comes back with rustling shade
And apple-blossoms fill the air—
I have a rendezvous with Death
When Spring brings back blue days and fair.

It may be he shall take my hand
And lead me into his dark land
And close my eyes and quench my breath—
It may be I shall pass him still.
I have a rendezvous with Death
On some scarred slope of battered hill,
When Spring comes round again this year
And the first meadow-flowers appear.

God knows 'twere better to be deep
Pillowed in silk and scented down,
Where Love throbs out in blissful sleep,
Pulse nigh to pulse, and breath to breath,
Where hushed awakenings are dear . . .
But I've a rendezvous with Death
At midnight in some flaming town,
When Spring trips north again this year,
And I to my pledged word am true,
I shall not fail that rendezvous.

TO MY BROTHER

Killed: Chaumont Wood, October, 1918

Louise Bogan

O you so long dead,
You masked and obscure,
I can tell you, all things endure:
The wine and the bread;

The marble quarried for the arch;
The iron become steel;
The spoke broken from the wheel;
The sweat of the long march;

The haystacks cut through like loaves,
And the hundred flowers from the seed.
All things indeed,
Though struck by the hooves

Of disaster, of time due,
Of fell loss and gain,
All things remain,
I can tell you, this is true,

Though burned down to stone,
Though lost from the eye,
I can tell you, and not lie—
Save of peace alone.

OVER THE TOP WITH PERSHING

Zelda Sayre Fitzgerald

The night was dark, the rain came down,
The boys stepped off with never a frown.
Into the trench all mud and slime,
And thousands of miles from their native clime.
They took their places in face of death,
And waited their turn with bated breath
    'Till the order came to open fire.
    They screwed their courage higher and higher.

Then the ready gunner with trigger cocked,
Let go the charge that the cannon rocked,
    And out of the mist a tongue of flame
    Across the darkness wrote his name.
"A red-haired gunner," the message read
As over the top a volley sped.
    And the khaki boys on victory bent
    Over the top with Pershing went.

Over the top they go to fight
For suffering friends and human right,
    Over the top they see their way
    To a clearer aim and a freer day,
Over the top, O God of Might,
Help our laddies to win the fight.

*U.S. Marine
and a French soldier,
France, World War I.
Defense Department Photograph
(Marine Corps).
U.S. Naval Institute, Annapolis*

CHAMPS D'HONNEUR

Ernest Hemingway

Soldiers never do die well;
    Crosses mark the places—
Wooden crosses where they fell,
    Stuck above their faces.

Soldiers pitch and cough and twitch—
    All the world roars red and black;
Soldiers smother in a ditch,
    Choking through the whole attack.

AMERICA'S WELCOME HOME

Henry Van Dyke

Oh, gallantly they fared forth in khaki and in blue,
America's crusading host of warriors bold and true;
They battled for the rights of man beside our brave Allies,
And now they're coming home to us with glory in their eyes.

    Oh, it's home again, and home again, America for me!
    Our hearts are turning home again and there we long to be,
    In our beautiful big country beyond the ocean bars,
    Where the air is full of sunlight and the flag is full of stars.

Our boys have seen the Old World as none have seen before.
They know the grisly horror of the German gods of war:
The noble faith of Britain and the hero-heart of France,
The soul of Belgium's fortitude and Italy's romance.

They bore our country's great word across the rolling sea,
"America swears brotherhood with all the just and free."
They wrote that word victorious on fields of mortal strife,
And many a valiant lad was proud to seal it with his life.

Oh, welcome home in Heaven's peace, dear spirits of the dead!
And welcome home ye living sons America hath bred!
The lords of war are beaten down, your glorious task is done;
You fought to make the whole world free, and the victory is won.

    Now it's home again, and home again, our hearts are turning west,
    Of all the lands beneath the sun America is best.
    We're going home to our own folks, beyond the ocean bars,
    Where the air is full of sunlight and the flag is full of stars.

Armistice Day, Wall Street, New York City.
Photograph, November 11, 1918. UPI/Bettmann Newsphotos

PART II

Map of My Country

from
MAP OF MY COUNTRY

John Holmes

A map of my native country is all edges,
The shore touching sea, the easy impartial rivers
Splitting the local boundary lines, round hills in two townships,
Blue ponds interrupting the careful county shapes.
The Mississippi runs down the middle. Cape Cod. The Gulf.
Nebraska is on latitude forty. Kansas is west of Missouri.

When I was a child, I drew it, from memory,
A game in the schoolroom, naming the big cities right.

Cloud shadows were not shown, nor where winter whitens,
Nor the wide road the day's wind takes.
None of the tall letters told my grandfather's name.
Nothing said, Here they see in clear air a hundred miles.
Here they go to bed early. They fear snow here.
Oak trees and maple boughs I had seen on the long hillsides
Changing color, and laurel, and bayberry, were never mapped.
Geography told only capitals and state lines.

I have come a long way using other men's maps for the turnings.
I have a long way to go.
It is time I drew the map again,
Spread with the broad colors of life, and words of my own
Saying, Here the people worked hard, and died for the wrong reasons.
Here wild strawberries tell the time of year.
I could not sleep, here, while bell-buoys beyond the surf rang.
Here trains passed in the night, crying of distance,
Calling to cities far away, listening for an answer.

On my own map of my own country
I shall show where there were never wars,
And plot the changed way I hear men speak in the west,
Words in the south slower, and food different.
Not the court-houses seen floodlighted at night from trains,
But the local stone built into housewalls,
And barns telling the traveler where he is
By the slant of the roof, the color of the paint.

Main Street.
Collage by Mick Wooten, 1968.
Courtesy the artist

Not monuments. Not the battlefields famous in school.
But Thoreau's pond, and Huckleberry Finn's island.
I shall name an unhistorical hill three boys climbed one morning.
Lines indicate my few journeys,
And the long way letters come from absent friends.

Forest is where green fern cooled me under the big trees.
Ocean is where I ran in the white drag of waves on white sand.
Music is what I heard in a country house while hearts broke,
Not knowing they were breaking, and Brahms wrote it.

All that I remember happened to me here.
This is the known world.
I shall make a star here for a man who died too young.
Here, and here, in gold, I shall mark two towns
Famous for nothing, except that I have been happy in them.

IN A PROMINENT BAR IN SECAUCUS ONE DAY   *X. J. Kennedy*
(To the tune of "The Old Orange Flute" or the tune of "Sweet Betsy from Pike")

In a prominent bar in Secaucus one day
Rose a lady in skunk with a topheavy sway,
Raised a knobby red finger—all turned from their beer—
While with eyes bright as snowcrust she sang high and clear:

"Now who of you'd think from an eyeload of me
That I once was a lady as proud as could be?
Oh I'd never sit down by a tumbledown drunk
If it wasn't, my dears, for the high cost of junk.

"All the gents used to swear that the white of my calf
Beat the down of a swan by a length and a half.
In the kerchief of linen I caught to my nose
Ah, there never fell snot, but a little gold rose.

"I had seven gold teeth and a toothpick of gold,
My Virginia cheroot was a leaf of it rolled
And I'd light it each time with a thousand in cash—
Why the bums used to fight if I flicked them an ash.

"Once the toast of the Biltmore, the belle of the Taft,
I would drink bottle beer at the Drake, never draft,
And dine at the Astor on Salisbury steak
With a clean tablecloth for each bite I did take.

"In a car like the Roxy I'd roll to the track,
A steel-guitar trio, a bar in the back,
And the wheels made no noise, they turned over so fast,
Still it took you ten minutes to see me go past.

"When the horses bowed down to me that I might choose,
I bet on them all, for I hated to lose.
Now I'm saddled each night for my butter and eggs
And the broken threads race down the backs of my legs.

"Let you hold in mind, girls, that your beauty must pass
Like a lovely white clover that rusts with its grass.
Keep your bottoms off barstools and marry you young
Or be left—an old barrel with many a bung.

"For when time takes you out for a spin in his car
You'll be hard-pressed to stop him from going too far
And be left by the roadside, for all your good deeds,
Two toadstools for tits and a face full of weeds."

All the house raised a cheer, but the man at the bar
Made a phonecall and up pulled a red patrol car
And she blew us a kiss as they copped her away
From that prominent bar in Secaucus, N.J.

Street Scene by Joe Jones.
1933. Oil on canvas.
National Museum of American Art,
Smithsonian Institution

from
THE LOVE SONG
OF J. ALFRED PRUFROCK

T. S. Eliot

Let us go then, you and I,
When the evening is spread out against the sky
Like a patient etherised upon a table;
Let us go, through certain half-deserted streets,
The muttering retreats
Of restless nights in one-night cheap hotels
And sawdust restaurants with oyster-shells:
Streets that follow like a tedious argument
Of insidious intent
To lead you to an overwhelming question. . .
Oh, do not ask, 'What is it?'
Let us go and make our visit.

In the room the women come and go
Talking of Michelangelo.

The yellow fog that rubs its back upon the window-panes,
The yellow smoke that rubs its muzzle on the window-panes,
Licked its tongue into the corners of the evening,
Lingered upon the pools that stand in drains,
Let fall upon its back the soot that falls from chimneys,
Slipped by the terrace, made a sudden leap,
And seeing that it was a soft October night,
Curled once about the house, and fell asleep.

And indeed there will be time
For the yellow smoke that slides along the street
Rubbing its back upon the window-panes;
There will be time, there will be time
To prepare a face to meet the faces that you meet;
There will be time to murder and create,
And time for all the works and days of hands
That lift and drop a question on your plate;
Time for you and time for me,
And time yet for a hundred indecisions,
And for a hundred visions and revisions,
Before the taking of a toast and tea.

THE ETERNAL RETURN

Robert Hillyer

Along how many Main Streets have I walked,
Greeting my friends, commenting on the weather,
Carrying bundles, wondering as I talked
If the brown paper bags would hold together—

At Christmastime with white breath blowing thin,
In spring when garden tidings are exchanged,
In autumn with the darkness closing in
And all the winter's work to be arranged.

Wherever I have lived—and many places
Have briefly seemed my permanent abode—
The shops on Main Street and the passing faces,
Beyond all history and change of mode,

Remain the same. And if, while on a walk,
I should encounter people who belong
In Main Streets of my past, I'd stop to talk
Without suspecting anything was wrong.

Even if I met someone who was dead,
I would discount the fact as in a dream.
Here things that lie behind are still ahead,
And calendars less final than they seem.

External accidents of time and space
Become, on Main Street, but illusory errors,
As all my incarnations, face to face,
Repeat themselves like people in two mirrors.

I greet acquaintances unchanged as I,
Stop for a moment, comment on the weather,
And at the corner, as I say goodbye,
Pray God my paper bundles hold together.

RIDING ON A STREETCAR WITH MY FATHER

Mary Ann Larkin

Riding on a streetcar with my father
I watch rows of hands clutching white circles
arms blocking noses
my father's fingers vanishing
behind a silver handle
the weave of his coat
even the cane of the seats
appearing and disappearing
The driver, black-suited
ringer of the bell
parts the dark

Pressing my nose against glass
I rub away the steam of my breath
see castles swirling in every window
globes melting into puddles
iridescent as pigeons' wings

My father's arm keeps me
from blending into the darkness
gliding on neon curves
my body a round dot
stretching to a single line of color
my father's sleeve a rough memory
my breath no longer staining the glass

The Green Car by William James Glackens.
1910. Oil on canvas.
The Metropolitan Museum of Art.
Arthur Hoppock Hearn Fund, 1937

TO BROOKLYN BRIDGE

Hart Crane

How many dawns, chill from his rippling rest
The seagull's wings shall dip and pivot him,
Shedding white rings of tumult, building high
Over the chained bay waters Liberty—

Then, with inviolate curve, forsake our eyes
As apparitional as sails that cross
Some page of figures to be filed away;
—Till elevators drop us from our day . . .

I think of cinemas, panoramic sleights
With multitudes bent toward some flashing scene
Never disclosed, but hastened to again,
Foretold to other eyes on the same screen;

And Thee, across the harbor, silver-paced
As though the sun took step of thee, yet left
Some motion ever unspent in thy stride,—
Implicitly thy freedom staying thee!

Out of some subway scuttle, cell or loft
A bedlamite speeds to thy parapets,
Tilting there momently, shrill shirt ballooning,
A jest falls from the speechless caravan.

Down Wall, from girder into street noon leaks,
A rip-tooth of the sky's acetylene;
All afternoon the cloud-flown derricks turn . . .
Thy cables breathe the North Atlantic still.

And obscure as that heaven of the Jews,
Thy guerdon . . . Accolade thou dost bestow
Of anonymity time cannot raise:
Vibrant reprieve and pardon thou dost show.

O harp and altar, of the fury fused,
(How could mere toil align thy choiring strings!)
Terrific threshold of the prophet's pledge,
Prayer of pariah, and the lover's cry,—

Again the traffic lights that skim thy swift
Unfractioned idiom, immaculate sigh of stars,
Beading thy path—condense eternity:
And we have seen night lifted in thine arms.

Under thy shadow by the piers I waited;
Only in darkness is thy shadow clear.
The City's fiery parcels all undone,
Already snow submerges an iron year . . .

O Sleepless as the river under thee,
Vaulting the sea, the prairies' dreaming sod,
Unto us lowliest sometime sweep, descend
And of the curveship lend a myth to God.

Brooklyn Bridge by Joseph Stella.
1917–18. Oil on canvas. Yale University Art Gallery, New Haven.
Gift of Collection Société Anonyme

BROADWAY

Carl Sandburg

I shall never forget you, Broadway
Your golden and calling lights.

I'll remember you long,
Tall-walled river of rush and play.

Hearts that know you hate you
And lips that have given you laughter
Have gone to their ashes of life and its roses,
Cursing the dreams that were lost
In the dust of your harsh and trampled stones.

A Raisin in the Sun.
PLAYBILL *for Lorraine Hansberry's award-winning play
featuring Sidney Poitier
at the Ethel Barrymore Theater,
New York City, 1958–59.*
PLAYBILL® is a registered trademark
of Playbill Incorporated, N.Y.C.,

HARLEM

Langston Hughes

What happens to a dream deferred?

Does it dry up
like a raisin in the sun?
Or fester like a sore—
And then run?
Does it stink like rotten meat?
Or crust and sugar over—
like a syrupy sweet?

Maybe it just sags
like a heavy load.

Or does it explode?

James Dean on Broadway.
© *Dennis Stock, Magnum Photos, Inc.*

A FIRE-TRUCK

Richard Wilbur

Right down the shocked street with a siren-blast
That sends all else skittering to the curb,
Redness, brass, ladders and hats hurl past,
　　Blurring to sheer verb,

Shift at the corner into uproarious gear
And make it around the turn in a squall of traction,
The headlong bell maintaining sure and clear,
　　Thought is degraded action!

Beautiful, heavy, unweary, loud, obvious thing!
I stand here purged of nuance, my mind a blank.
All I was brooding upon has taken wing,
　　And I have you to thank.

As you howl beyond hearing I carry you into my mind,
Ladders and brass and all, there to admire
Your phoenix-red simplicity, enshrined
　　In that not extinguished fire.

THE GREAT FIGURE

William Carlos Williams

Among the rain
and lights
I saw the figure 5
in gold
on a red
firetruck
moving
tense
unheeded
to gong clangs
siren howls
and wheels rumbling
through the dark city.

I Saw the Figure 5 in Gold
by Charles Demuth. 1928.
Oil on composition board.
The painting is based on the poem
by William Carlos Williams.
The Metropolitan Museum of Art.
Alfred Stieglitz Collection

EAGER STREET

Kendra Kopelke

I drag my shirt across the floor
with my foot, kick the shoes
under the couch and everything
is out of order. Even the goldfish
plant is growing in wrong directions,
its pot too close to the window,
leaves rotting on the sill to dust.
Everyone knows the women in Baltimore
wash their front steps each week.
On their knees, on Saturday,
they rub their palms hard against
the marble, as their children play
together on the sidewalk. But you and I
share another kind of order,
when you're gone, I can see
where you've been, which towel
you dried your hair with, what magazine
you read at dinner. Some weeks
we barely speak, but if we're lucky,
by morning our bodies drift together,
our talk curls to the center of the bed
like a daughter. And the clothes
covering the furniture are forgiven.

Forgiven, yet still not put away,
it's how we live through each
unfolding season. We drive
our guests down Eager Street,
point out the marble stairs,
the strong women, the generations
of commitment. It's a good story.
These things out of order make
a difference. There is a dream
inside each glass on the dresser,
each book on the floor. Cleaning
would be a lie.

But tonight, I remember back
to our first winter on a southern coast,
you were picking the beach clean
of shells, stuffing them in your pocket,
you were just a little ahead of me
when you spotted a flat shell shaped
like a fish and you tossed it hard
into the waves. You kept your back
to me a long time. You must have been
wishing hard then, for something
like our lives, to matter.

Still Life Painting 30 by Tom Wesselmann. 1963.
Assemblage, oil, enamel, and synthetic polymer paint
on composition board with collage of printed advertisements,
plastic artificial flowers, refrigerator door,
plastic replicas of 7-Up bottles,
glazed and framed color reproduction,
and stamped metal, 48 ½ × 66 × 4″.
Collection, The Museum of Modern Art, New York.
Gift of Philip Johnson

CHICAGO

Carl Sandburg

> Hog Butcher for the World,
> Tool Maker, Stacker of Wheat,
> Player with Railroads and the Nation's Freight Handler;
> Stormy, husky, brawling,
> City of the Big Shoulders:

They tell me you are wicked and I believe them, for I have seen your
    painted women under the gas lamps luring the farm boys.
And they tell me you are crooked and I answer: Yes, it is true I have seen
    the gunman kill and go free to kill again.
And they tell me you are brutal and my reply is: On the faces of women
    and children I have seen the marks of wanton hunger.
And having answered so I turn once more to those who sneer at this my city,
    and I give them back the sneer and say to them:
Come and show me another city with lifted head singing so proud to be
    alive and coarse and strong and cunning.
Flinging magnetic curses amid the toil of piling job on job, here is a tall bold
    slugger set vivid against the little soft cities;
Fierce as a dog with tongue lapping for action, cunning as a savage pitted
    against the wilderness,
> Bareheaded,
> Shoveling,
> Wrecking,
> Planning,
> Building, breaking, rebuilding,
Under the smoke, dust all over his mouth, laughing with white teeth,
Under the terrible burden of destiny laughing as a young man laughs,
Laughing even as an ignorant fighter laughs who has never lost a battle,
Bragging and laughing that under his wrist is the pulse, and under his ribs the
    heart of the people,
> > Laughing!
Laughing the stormy, husky, brawling laughter of Youth, half-naked, sweating,
    proud to be Hog Butcher, Tool Maker, Stacker of Wheat, Player with
    Railroads and Freight Handler to the Nation.

McDONALD'S, NEW HARTFORD, NY

Valerie Worth

They expanded
The Seneca Turnpike McDonald's
Some years ago, so now
There are tables inside.

But one can still eat in the car,
In March,
Parked by the storage shed, facing
A pile of black snow
That will glint like coal if the sun
Shines.

The long curb has
Cracked edges; a stray pebble stands
Revealed;
A ridge of mud, shaved up by the
Snowplow, thaws
Near the waste bin.

Behind a wire fence
Somebody's back yard keeps
An apple tree and a couple of tough
Lilacs, all
Waving their March buds
At McDonald's, singing
Their seasonal paeans.

Over 17 Billion Served
by R. O. Blechman.
March 1974,
in Architecture Plus.
Ink on paper.
Library of Congress

TRAVELING TO TOWN

Duane BigEagle

When I was very young
we always went to town
in the wagon.
We'd leave as soon
as the day's first heat
had stopped the mare's breath
from forming a cloud
in the air.
As we rode down main street
the town revealed itself
backwards
for my sister and I to see.
We loved the brick and sandstone buildings
and the farmer's market
with its sawdust floor.
Best of all
was Monkey Ward
with its large center room
and the little wires
with paper messages
that flew back and forth
like trained birds.
We finally got to Safeway
where Grandma did the shopping
and Grandpa sat outside
on the brick steps in the sunlight
watching all the grandkids.
From a shady coolness
on the other side of the street
the ice cream store
would call us
with its banging screen door.
Grandpa always had money for ice cream
and we'd ride home down main street
licking ice cream
watching the town reveal itself
backwards again
in afternoon sun.

A STATE OF NATURE

John Hollander

```
                                    Some broken
                                  Iroquois adze
                                pounded southward
                                and resembled this
                              outline once But now
                             boundaries foul-lines
                            and even sea-coasts are
                            naturally involved with
                            mappers and followers of
                          borders So that we who grew
                        up here might think That steak is
            shaped too much like New York to be real And like
          the shattered flinty implement whose ghost lives
             inside our sense of what this rough chunk should
             by right of history recall the language spoken by
            its shapers now inhabits only streams and lakes and
          hills The natural names are only a chattering and mean
        only the land they label How shall we live in a forest of
                                such murmurs with
                                 no ideas but in
                                forms a state
                                 whose name
                                    passes
                                      for
                                       a city
```

113

Exploring the Country

CROSSING KANSAS
BY TRAIN

Donald Justice

The telephone poles
have been holding their
arms out
a long time now
to birds
that will not
settle there
but pass with
strange cawings
westward to
where dark trees
gather about
a waterhole. This
is Kansas. The
mountains start here
just behind
the closed eyes
of a farmer's
sons asleep
in their workclothes.

THREE KINDS OF PLEASURES

Robert Bly

Sometimes, riding in a car, in Wisconsin
Or Illinois, you notice those dark telephone poles
One by one lift themselves out of the fence line
And slowly leap on the gray sky—
And past them the snowy fields.

The darkness drifts down like snow on the picked cornfields
In Wisconsin, and on these black trees
Scattered, one by one,
Through the winter fields—
We see stiff weeds and brownish stubble,
And white snow left now only in the wheeltracks of the combine.

It is a pleasure, also, to be driving
Toward Chicago, near dark,
And see the lights in the barns.
The bare trees more dignified than ever,
Like a fierce man on his deathbed,
And the ditches along the road half full of a private snow.

Railroad Sunset by Edward Hopper.
1929. Oil on canvas.
Whitney Museum of American Art, New York

OUT WHERE THE WEST BEGINS

Arthur Chapman

Out where the hand-clasp's a little stronger,
Out where the smile dwells a little longer,
   That's where the West begins;
Out where the sun is a little brighter,
Where the snows that fall are a trifle whiter,
Where the bonds of home are a wee bit tighter,
   That's where the West begins.

Out where the skies are a little bluer,
Out where friendship's a little truer,
   That's where the West begins;
Out where a fresher breeze is blowing,
Where there's laughter in every streamlet flowing,
Where there's more of reaping and less of sowing,
   That's where the West begins.

Out where the world is in the making,
Where fewer hearts in despair are aching,
   That's where the West begins;
Where there's more of singing and less of sighing,
Where there's more of giving and less of buying,
And a man makes friends without half trying
   That's where the West begins.

I GO DREAMING ROADS IN MY YOUTH

Luis Omar Salinas

I'm not interested in the poverty
of ignorance and its songs,
to be generous to myself is my song;
I will give my shirt to no one
even though I talk too much and
give my words to the ungrateful
they will not find a home in my thoughts.

I put on my hat, stride forward,
act, dream, love; I take a drink
and let fame touch me, yet in the end
I'll place it to rest.

When I raise my arm to the populace
I raise it with sincerity
and pride in my monstrous vitality.
When the world clubs me
I shall fight back, if it loves me
I will love back, if it steps in my
shadow's fortune, I will give thanks
to God and those who surround me.

I have many stories, a haughty dramatist
weaving scenes of optimism, of alegria,
of romance. The world is too tired
and little concerned with pathos or
the consequences of tragedy.

What is important is the eloquence
of a river and a boy pushing a boat
into the water, a white dove gently
from the hands of his mother and
a clumsy serenade dreaming the afternoon.

Today, I like this world, and
if your life is worth nothing, don't sing,
don't come to my door with broken hearts
and complaints. Today, I go dreaming
roads in my youth.

SUNSET FROM OMAHA HOTEL WINDOW

Carl Sandburg

Into the blue river hills
The red sun runners go
And the long sand changes
And today is a goner
And today is not worth haggling over.

    Here in Omaha
    The gloaming is bitter
    As in Chicago
    Or Kenosha.

The long sand changes.
Today is a goner.
Time knocks in another brass nail.
Another yellow plunger shoots the dark.

    Constellations
    Wheeling over Omaha
    As in Chicago
    Or Kenosha.

The long sand is gone
        and all the talk is stars.
They circle in a dome over Nebraska.

Pottery bowl, Zia Pueblo.
Denver Art Museum

SOUTH TEXAS SUMMER RAIN

Rebecca Gonzales

Dust cools easily
with the lightest summer rain.
Not rocks.
In the midst of dry brush,
they hold the sun like a match,
a threat to the water
that would wear them out.

Dust becomes clay,
cups rain like an innocent offering.
Not rocks.
They round their backs to the rain,
channel it down the street where children play,
feeling the rocks they walk on,
sharp as ever under the water,
streaming away.

If rocks hold water at all,
it's only long enough
for a cactus to grow gaudy flowers,
hoard a cheap drink,
flash it like a sin
worth the pain.

POEM FOR ARIZONA

Marcia Spriggs

Rocking lazy
against the metal of the swing,
digging my toes into the sand
to scatter pebbles and ants,
I look up, squinting, to see
a distant painting without edges.
Deep purple black ridges
and a smooth blue sky.
High above the black
a small gray smear, fingerprint
touched before the paint was dry.
"It's raining in the mountains, Marcy,
It's raining in the mountains."

THANKSGIVING AT SNAKE BUTTE

James Welch

In time we rode that trail
up the butte as far as time
would let us. The answer to our time
lay hidden in the long grasses
on the top. Antelope scattered

through the rocks before us, clattered
unseen down the easy slope to the west.
Our horses balked, stiff-legged,
their nostrils flared at something unseen
gliding smoothly through brush away.

On top, our horses broke, loped through
a small stand of stunted pine, then jolted
to a nervous walk. Before us lay
the smooth stones of our ancestors, the fish,
the lizard, snake and bent-kneed

bowman—etched by something crude,
by a wandering race, driven by their names
for time: its winds, its rain, its snow
and the cold moon tugging at the crude figures
in this, the season of their loss.

118

The Blue Mesa
by *Nora Frenkel.*
Watercolor.
Courtesy Hirschl and Adler Galleries, New York

JULY IN INDIANA

Robert Fitzgerald

The wispy cuttings lie in rows
                where mowers passed in the heat.
A parching scent enters the nostrils.

Morning barely breathed before
                noon mounted on tiers of maples,
fiery and still. The eye smarts.

Moisture starts on the back of the hand.

Gloss and chrome on burning cars fan out
cobwebby lightning over children
                damp and flushed in the shade.

Over all the back yards, locusts
buzz like little sawmills in the trees,
                or is the song ecstatic?—rising
rising until it gets tired and dies away.

Grass baking, prickling sweat, great blazing tree,
magical shadow and cicada song
                recall
those heroes that in ancient days, reclining
on roots and hummocks, tossing pen-knives,
                delved in earth's cool underworld
and lightly squeezed the black clot from the blade.

Evening came, will come with lucid stillness
                printed by the distinct cricket
and, far off, by the freight cars' coupling clank.

                A warm full moon will rise
out of the mothering dust, out of the dry corn land.

THE CLOSING OF THE RODEO

William Jay Smith

The lariat snaps; the cowboy rolls
    His pack, and mounts and rides away.
Back to the land the cowboy goes.

Plumes of smoke from the factory sway
    In the setting sun. The curtain falls,
A train in the darkness pulls away.

Good-by, says the rain on the iron roofs.
    Good-by, say the barber poles.
Dark drum the vanishing horses' hooves.

The Bronco Buster
1895. Bronze.
National Cowboy Hall of Fame Collection, Oklahoma City

THE PLACE FOR NO STORY

Robinson Jeffers

The coast hills at Sovranes Creek:
No trees, but dark scant pasture drawn thin
Over rock shaped like flame;
The old ocean at the land's foot, the vast
Gray extension beyond the long white violence;
A herd of cows and the bull
Far distant, hardly apparent up the dark slope;
And the gray air haunted with hawks:
This place is the noblest thing I have ever seen.
    No imaginable
Human presence here could do anything
But dilute the lonely self-watchful passion.

121

CALIFORNIA WINTER

Karl Shapiro

It is winter in California, and outside
Is like the interior of a florist shop:
A chilled and moisture-laden crop
Of pink camellias lines the path; and what
Rare roses for a banquet or a bride,
So multitudinous that they seem a glut!

A line of snails crosses the golf-green lawn
From the rosebushes to the ivy bed;
An arsenic compound is distributed
For them. The gardener will rake up the shells
And leave in a corner of the patio
The little mound of empty snails, like skulls.

By noon the fog is burnt off by the sun
And the world's immensest sky opens a page
For the exercises of a future age;
Now jet planes draw straight lines, parabolas,
And x's, which the wind, before they're done,
Erases leisurely or pulls to fuzz.

It is winter in the valley of the vine.
The vineyards crucified on stakes suggest
War cemeteries, but the fruit is pressed,
The redwood vats are brimming in the shed,
And on the sidings stand tank cars of wine,
For which bright juice a billion grapes have bled.

And skiers from the snow line driving home
Descend through almond orchards, olive farms,
Fig tree and palm tree—everything that warms
The imagination of the wintertime.
If the walls were older one would think of Rome:
If the land were stonier one would think of Spain.

But this land grows the oldest living things,
Trees that were young when Pharaohs ruled the world,
Trees whose new leaves are only just unfurled.
Beautiful they are not; they oppress the heart
With gigantism and with immortal wings;
And yet one feels the sumptuousness of this dirt.

It is raining in California, a straight rain
Cleaning the heavy oranges on the bough,
Filling the gardens till the gardens flow,
Shining the olives, tiling the gleaming tile,
Waxing the dark camellia leaves more green,
Flooding the daylong valleys like the Nile.

SLEEP
IN THE MOJAVE DESERT

Sylvia Plath

Out here there are no hearthstones,
Hot grains, simply. It is dry, dry.
And the air dangerous. Noonday acts queerly
On the mind's eye, erecting a line
Of poplars in the middle distance, the only
Object beside the mad, straight road
One can remember men and houses by.
A cool wind should inhabit those leaves
And a dew collect on them, dearer than money,
In the blue hour before sunup.
Yet they recede, untouchable as tomorrow,
Or those glittery fictions of spilt water
That glide ahead of the very thirsty.

I think of the lizards airing their tongues
In the crevice of an extremely small shadow
And the toad guarding his heart's droplet.
The desert is white as a blind man's eye,
Comfortless as salt. Snake and bird
Doze behind the old masks of fury.
We swelter like firedogs in the wind.
The sun puts its cinder out. Where we lie
The heat-cracked crickets congregate
In their black armorplate and cry.
The day-moon lights up like a sorry mother,
And the crickets come creeping into our hair
To fiddle the short night away.

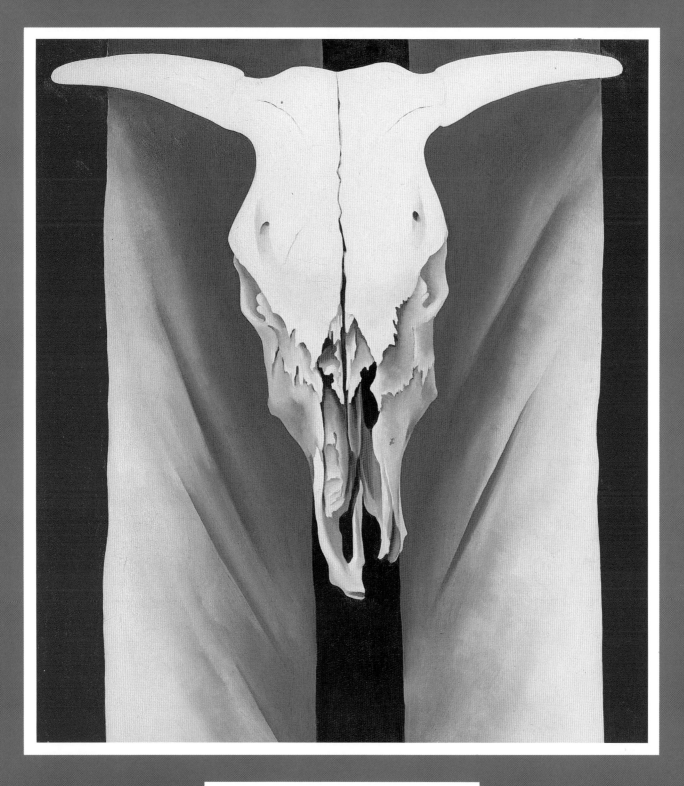

Cow's Skull—Red White and Blue
by Georgia O'Keeffe.
1931. Oil on canvas.
The Metropolitan Museum of Art.
The Alfred Stieglitz Collection

CROSSING NATION   *Allen Ginsberg*

Under silver wing
    San Francisco's towers sprouting
                thru thin gas clouds,
    Tamalpais black-breasted above Pacific azure
        Berkeley hills pine-covered below—
Dr Leary in his brown house scribing Independence
                            Declaration
        typewriter at window
    silver panorama in natural eyeball—

Sacramento valley rivercourse's Chinese
        dragonflames licking green flats north-hazed
    State Capitol metallic rubble, dry checkered fields
      to Sierras—past Reno, Pyramid Lake's
      blue Altar, pure water in Nevada sands'
        brown wasteland scratched by tires

      Jerry Rubin arrested! Beaten, jailed,
           coccyx broken—
Leary out of action—"a public menace . . .
      persons of tender years . . . immature
          judgment . . . psychiatric examination . . ."
i.e. Shut up or Else   Loonybin or Slam

Leroi on bum gun rap, $7,000
      lawyer fees, years' negotiations—
SPOCK GUILTY headlined temporary, Joan Baez'
      paramour husband Dave Harris to Gaol
Dylan silent on politics, & safe—
      having a baby, a man—
Cleaver shot at, jail'd, maddened, parole revoked,
Vietnam War flesh-heap grows higher,
      blood splashing down the mountains of bodies
        on to Cholon's sidewalks—
Blond boys in airplane seats fed technicolor
      Murderers advance w/ Death-chords
        thru photo basement,
    Earplugs in, steak on plastic
        served—Eyes up to the Image—

What do I have to lose if America falls?
    my body? my neck? my personality?

Jack Kerouac.
Photograph by Allen Ginsberg.
Kerouac (1922–69) along with Ginsberg
chronicled the Beat Generation,
and is known for his novels On the Road *(1957)*
and Desolation Angels *(1965).*

MARIN

Philip Booth

Marin
saw how it feels:
the first raw shock
of Labrador current,
the surfacing gasp
at jut of rock,
bent sails, and wedged
trees. He wrote it—
Stonington, Small
Point, and Cape Split—
through a pane so
cracked by the lode-
star sun that he
swam back, blinded,
into himself, to
sign the after-
image: initialled
mountains, ledged
towns white as
Machias after
the hayrake rain,
sun-splintered
water, and written
granite—dark light
unlike what you
ever saw, until,
inland, your own
eyes close and, out
of that sea change,
islands rise thick,
like the riptide
paint that, flooding,
tugs at your vitals,
and is more Maine
than Maine.

Deer Isle—Marine Fantasy by John Marin.
1917. Watercolor.
The artist is the subject of Philip Booth's poem, opposite page.
Honolulu Academy of Arts. Purchase, 1966

STORM WARNINGS

Adrienne Rich

The glass has been falling all the afternoon,
And knowing better than the instrument

What winds are walking overhead, what zone
Of gray unrest is moving across the land,
I leave the book upon a pillowed chair
And walk from window to closed window, watching
Boughs strain against the sky

And think again, as often when the air
Moves inward toward a silent core of waiting,
How with a single purpose time has traveled
By secret currents of the undiscerned
Into this polar realm. Weather abroad
And weather in the heart alike come on
Regardless of prediction.

Between foreseeing and averting change
Lies all the mastery of elements
Which clocks and weatherglasses cannot alter.
Time in the hand is not control of time,
Nor shattered fragments of an instrument
A proof against the wind; the wind will rise,
We can only close the shutters.

I draw the curtains as the sky goes black
And set a match to candles sheathed in glass
Against the keyhole draught, the insistent whine
Of weather through the unsealed aperture.
This is our sole defense against the season;
These are the things that we have learned to do
Who live in troubled regions.

MARINA

O. B. Hardison, Jr.

I think of the sea changing and changing.
There is a long swell moving in from the Azores
Awash on the gray sand.
The sky unfolds into the water.
At Holden, Long Beach, Wilmington, Ocean Isle, Hatteras, Nags Head
The Outer Banks are ringing with explosions of light.
Clouds blossom in the water and the shore flames with the glory of their opening
As though God were making the world again.
Here I am, where the gentle sea touches the land,
And every name is new,
And every name is another name for the sea.

Girl with Shell at Ear by Winslow Homer. 1880.
Gouache and charcoal over graphite on gray paper.
Worcester Art Museum,
Massachusetts. Bequest of Grenville H. Norcross

from
THE DRY SALVAGES

T. S. Eliot

I do not know much about gods; but I think that the river
Is a strong brown god—sullen, untamed and intractable,
Patient to some degree, at first recognised as a frontier;
Useful, untrustworthy, as a conveyor of commerce;
Then only a problem confronting the builder of bridges.
The problem once solved, the brown god is almost forgotten
By the dwellers in cities—ever, however, implacable,
Keeping his seasons and rages, destroyer, reminder
Of what men choose to forget. Unhonoured, unpropitiated
By worshippers of the machine, but waiting, watching and waiting.
His rhythm was present in the nursery bedroom,
In the rank ailanthus of the April dooryard,
In the smell of grapes on the autumn table,
And the evening circle in the winter gaslight.

The river is within us, the sea is all about us;
The sea is the land's edge also, the granite
Into which it reaches, the beaches where it tosses
Its hints of earlier and other creation:
The starfish, the hermit crab, the whale's backbone;
The pools where it offers to our curiosity
The more delicate algae and the sea anemone.
It tosses up our losses, the torn seine,
The shattered lobsterpot, the broken oar
And the gear of foreign dead men. The sea has many voices,
Many gods and many voices.

OLD SAILOR LOOKING
AT A CONTAINER SHIP

Robert Carson

At bend of bay
Sail voices in the wind
Fog's slow spiral under the bridge
He sees containers overall.
All the same shape, all the same size.
Loaded from a flat obtrusive yard;
Cut from the city by cyclone fencing.

He remembers sixty years ago,
Time cutting through him
Like a knife.
Silver blade clear as
Light on the open sea;
And against the horizon
Canvas wings
Beating down the sky.

Schinz's Sandpiper
Plate 335 in The Birds of America, *lithographed by J. T. Bowen of Philadelphia,*
after the original painting by John Jay Audubon, 1871

SANDPIPER   *Elizabeth Bishop*

The roaring alongside he takes for granted,
and that every so often the world is bound to shake.
He runs, he runs to the south, finical, awkward,
in a state of controlled panic, a student of Blake.

The beach hisses like fat. On his left, a sheet
of interrupting water comes and goes
and glazes over his dark and brittle feet.
He runs, he runs straight through it, watching his toes.

—Watching, rather, the spaces of sand between them,
where (no detail too small) the ocean drains
rapidly backwards and downwards. As he runs,
he stares at the dragging grains.

The world is a mist. The world is marvellously
minute and vast and clear. The tide
is higher or lower. He couldn't tell you which,
His beak is focussed; he is preoccupied,

looking for something, something, something.
Poor bird, he is obsessed!
The millions of grains are black, white, tan, and gray,
and mixed with quartz grains, rose and amethyst.

131

THE MOUTH OF THE HUDSON

(For Esther Brooks)

Robert Lowell

A single man stands like a bird-watcher,
and scuffles the pepper and salt snow
from a discarded, gray
Westinghouse Electric cable drum.
He cannot discover America by counting
the chains of condemned freight-trains
from thirty states. They jolt and jar
and junk in the siding below him.
He has trouble with his balance.
His eyes drop,
and he drifts with the wild ice
ticking seaward down the Hudson,
like the blank sides of a jig-saw puzzle.

The ice ticks seaward like a clock.
A Negro toasts
wheat-seeds over the coke-fumes
of a punctured barrel.
Chemical air
sweeps in from New Jersey.
and smells of coffee.

Across the river,
ledges of suburban factories tan
in the sulphur-yellow sun
of the unforgiveable landscape.

MAX SCHMITT
IN A SINGLE SCULL

Richmond Lattimore

How shall the river learn
its winter look, steel and brown, how shall we
upon our moving mirror here discern
the way light falls on bridge and bare tree
except as in the painting? Cold fires burn

autumn into winter. Here still
the pencilled sculls dip, precise arms beat
the water-circles of their progress. Skill
arrowheads elegance. City Line to 30th Street
is forever, Eakins, your Schuylkill

and ours. What you have done
made us see what we saw. Thus our eyes
after your image catch the steel and brown
of rowers on the water, improvise
by you our colors in the winter sun.

132

Max Schmitt in a Single Scull by Thomas Eakins. 1871.
Oil on canvas.
The painting inspired the poem by Richmond Lattimore on the opposite page.
The Metropolitan Museum of Art.
Alfred N. Punnett Fund and Gift of George D. Pratt, 1934

THE NEGRO SPEAKS OF RIVERS

Langston Hughes

I've known rivers:
I've known rivers ancient as the world and older than the flow of human
     blood in human veins.

My soul has grown deep like the rivers.

I bathed in the Euphrates when dawns were young.
I built my hut near the Congo and it lulled me to sleep.

I looked upon the Nile and raised the pyramids above it.
I heard the singing of the Mississippi when Abe Lincoln went down
     to New Orleans, and I've seen its muddy bosom turn all golden in
     the sunset.

I've known rivers:
Ancient, dusky rivers.

My soul has grown deep like the rivers.

Eel Spearing at Setauket by William Sidney Mount.
1845. Oil on canvas.
New York State Historical Association, Cooperstown

In Search Of

COVERED BRIDGE

Robert Penn Warren

Another land, another age, another self
Before all had happened that has happened since
And is now arranged on the shelf
Of memory in a sequence that I call Myself.

How can you think back and know
Who was the boy, sleepless, who lay
In a moonless night of summer, but with star-glow
Gemming the dewy miles, and acres, you used to go?

You think of starlight on the river, star
By star declaring its motionless, holy self,
Except at the riffle by the sandbar.
You wondered if reflection was seen by the sky's star.

Long, long ago, some miles away,
There was an old covered bridge across that stream,
And if impact of hoof or wheel made the loose boards sway,
That echo wandered the landscape, night or day.

But if by day, the human bumble and grind
Absorbed the sound, or even birdsong
Interfered in its fashion, and only at night might you find
That echo filling the vastness of your mind,

Till you wondered what night, long off, you would set hoof
On those loose boards and then proceed
To trot through the caverning dark beneath that roof.
Going where? Just going. That would be enough.

Then silence would wrap that starlit land,
And you would sleep—who now do not sleep
As you wonder why you cannot understand
What pike, highway, or path has led you from land to land,

From year to year, to lie in what strange room,
Where to prove identity you now lift up
Your own hand—scarcely visible in that gloom.

THIS PLACE IN THE WAYS

Muriel Rukeyser

Having come to this place
I set out once again
on the dark and marvelous way
from where I began:
belief in the love of the world,
woman, spirit, and man.

Having failed in all things
I enter a new age
seeing the old ways as toys,
the houses of a stage
painted and long forgot;
and I find love and rage.

Rage for the world as it is
but for what it may be
more love now than last year
and always less self-pity
since I know in a clearer light
the strength of the mystery.

And at this place in the ways
I wait for song.
My poem-hand still, on the paper,
all night long.
Poems in throat and hand, asleep,
and my storm beating strong!

Gertrude Stein *by Pablo Picasso.*
1906. Oil on canvas.
The Metropolitan Museum of Art.
Bequest of Gertrude Stein, 1946

from PORTRAITS AND REPETITION   *Gertrude Stein*

How do you like what you have.

This is a question that anybody can ask anybody.
Ask it.

In asking it I began to make portraits of anybody.

How do you like what you have is one way of having
an important thing to ask of any one.

That is essentially the portrait of any one, one
portrait of any one.

I began to think about portraits of any one.

If they are themselves inside them what are they
and what has it to do with what they do.

137

NIGHTS ALONG THE RIVER

Charles Sullivan

Nights along the river,
Near the boats,
With all our conversations
Floating past,
I stay awake to hear
A thousand-throated chorus
Of the geese home-
Coming from their summers
In the north.

While I wait I wonder
What they feel and what
They celebrate—another flight
From radiance to radiance,
Another triumph of successful
Navigation by consensus,
Or the simple repossession
Of this river and these farms
For one more winter of survival?

Tonight or some night soon,
By star or moonlight, when you
Are sleeping far removed from here
And I am proving I don't need your love,
The geese will fight their windy way
Across the bay and up the river
To this cove, and their voices
Will call the dreamer out of me
To rejoice with them.

I will see their patterns
Change from stream to circle,
The boisterous leaders finding range
As they descend, the others gliding
Wing on wing behind them, winding down,
Spiral after spiral, steeper, steeper,
Until they must release the beaten air
And settle in. The river will accept them.
Then, if three or four keep watch, I know
The rest and I can sleep.

Maryland, Eastern Shore.
Photograph by M. E. Warren.
Copyright by M.E. Warren.

SNOWBANKS NORTH OF THE HOUSE

Robert Bly

Those great sweeps of snow that stop suddenly six feet from the house . . .
Thoughts that go so far.
The boy gets out of high school and reads no more books;
the son stops calling home.
The mother puts down her rolling pin and makes no more bread.
And the wife looks at her husband one night at a party and loves him no more.
The energy leaves the wine, and the minister falls leaving the church.
It will not come closer—
the one inside moves back, and the hands touch nothing, and are safe.

And the father grieves for his son, and will not leave the room where
    the coffin stands;
he turns away from his wife, and she sleeps alone.

And the sea lifts and falls all night; the moon goes on through the
    unattached heavens alone.
And the toe of the shoe pivots
in the dust. . . .
The man in the black coat turns, and goes back down the hill.
No one knows why he came, or why he turned away, and did not climb the hill.

Women and Dog *by Marisol. 1964.*
Fur, leather, plaster, synthetic polymer, wood.
Whitney Museum of American Art, New York.
Gift of the Friends of the Whitney Museum of American Art

NOT SAYING MUCH   *Linda Gregg*

My father is dead and there is nothing left
now except ashes and a few photographs.
The men are together in the old pictures.
Two generations of them working and boxing
and playing fiddles. They were interested
mostly in how men were men. Muscle and size.
Played their music for women and the women
did not. The music of women was long ago.
Being together made the men believe somehow.
Something the United States of America could
not give them. Not even the Mississippi.
Not running away or the Civil War or farming
the plains. Not exploring or the dream of gold.
The music and standing that way together
seems to have worked. They married women
the way they made a living. And the women
married them back, without saying much,
not loving much, not singing ever.
Those I knew in California lived and died
in beauty and not enough money. But the beauty
was like a face with the teeth touching
under closed lips and the eyes still. The men
did not talk to them much, and neither time
nor that fine place gave them a sweetness.

THE ROAD NOT TAKEN

Robert Frost

Two roads diverged in a yellow wood,
And sorry I could not travel both
And be one traveler, long I stood
And looked down one as far as I could
To where it bent in the undergrowth;

Then took the other, as just as fair,
And having perhaps the better claim,
Because it was grassy and wanted wear;
Though as for that, the passing there
Had worn them really about the same,

And both that morning equally lay
In leaves no step had trodden black.
Oh, I kept the first for another day!
Yet knowing how way leads on to way,
I doubted if I should ever come back.

I shall be telling this with a sigh
Somewhere ages and ages hence:
Two roads diverged in a wood, and I—
I took the one less traveled by,
And that has made all the difference.

Martin Luther King, Jr.
Photograph of King in a Jefferson County
Courthouse jail cell, Birmingham, 1967.
UPI/Bettmann Newsphotos

AUDEN AT MILWAUKEE

Stephen Spender

Dined with Auden. He'd been at Milwaukee
Three days, talking to the students.
'They loved me. They were entranced.'
His face lit up the scene.
I saw there the picture of him, crammed into
Carpet bag clothes and carpet slippers
His face alone alive alone above them.
He must have negotiated himself into the room
Like an object, a prize, a gift that knows his worth,
Measuring his value out to them on scales,
Word weighed by word, absorbed in his own voice.
He knows they're young and, better, that he's old.
He shares his distance from them like a joke.
They love him for it. This, because they feel
That he belongs to none, yet gives to all.
They see him as an object, artefact, that time
Has ploughed criss-cross with all these lines
Yet has a core within that purely burns.

Chart, 1943,
by W. H. Auden
for a seminar
on Romanticism
at Swarthmore College,
Pennsylvania.
Henry W. and
Albert A. Berg Collection.
The New York Public Library.
Astor, Lenox and
Tilden Foundations

A HEALTHY SPOT

W. H. Auden

They're nice—one would never dream of going over
Any contract of theirs with a magnifying
Glass, or of locking up one's letters —also
Kind and efficient—one gets what one asks for.
Just what is wrong, then, that, living among them,
One is constantly struck by the number of
Happy marriages and unhappy people?
They attend all the lectures on Post-War Problems,
For they do mind, they honestly want to help; yet,
As they notice the earth in their morning papers,
What sense do they make of its folly and horror
Who have never, one is convinced, felt a sudden
Desire to torture the cat or do a strip-tease
In a public place? Have they ever, one wonders,
Wanted so much to see a unicorn, even
A dead one? Probably. But they won't say so,
Ignoring by tacit consent our hunger
For eternal life, that caged rebuked question
Occasionally let out at clambakes or
College reunions, and which the smoking-room story
Alone, ironically enough, stands up for.

Eden = The World = Paradise
Essential Being
↓
The Fall

Search for salvation
by return to Nature
The Pure Deed

This world
Knowledge of Good and Evil
Dualism of experience
Existential Being

Search for salvation by
return from Nature
The Pure Word

Hell of the Pure Deed
Power without Purpose

Hell 1
The Pure Word. Knowledge without will.

	Sea	Forest	City	Mountains	Desert
Main Symbol	Sea	Forest	City	Mountains	Desert
Secondary Symbols	Blood. Tears. Serpents. Fish	Cold beasts	People	Birds. Aeroplanes. Automobiles etc. Insects. Geometrical shapes. Bones	
Myth Symbols	Dragons. Sirens. Rheingold	Giants. Dwarfs		Heroes & gods. Glaciers. Ghosts	
	The Golden Fleece		The Ring		The Magicians castle
Metaphysical condition	Pure Aesthetic Immediacy. Ethical non-becoming	Soul. Actualisation of the Possible. Spirit. Art ethical becoming aesthetic being		Pure Ethical Being. Aesthetic nonentity	
Order	Monist Unity (water). Barbaric vagueness	Differentiated Diversity in Unity. Country (village) Civilisation (Town)		Disorderly Multiplicity (sand-grains) Decadent Triviality	
Kind of Time	Natural cyclical. Nunc-stehe. Everlasting change (The circle)	Historical. Irreversible. Process change (Rapid)		Static eternal. Non changing (The turbine)	
Relation of objects occasions	Mutual Irresponsibility	Conscious relations (The void) (The contract)		Mutual Aversion	
Relation to self	self-sufficiency	Vertical Vulgar self-deception. Blind Eros. Voyeur Celeste		self-negation	
Requiredness	objective unconscious (Determinism)	subjective		Conscious lack of Requiredness (Paralysis of Indecision)	
Intended size	Sensuality	Criminals Bohemians ←(Anxiety)→ Politicians Bourgeois Pharisees		Pride	
Psychology	Stream of sensations	Sensation. Intuitive. Intuitive. Sensation / Feeling. Thinking. Thinking. Feeling		Abstract logic	
Diseases	Cancer	Digestive. Venereal	Sensory Respiratory	} Paralysis	
Mental Diseases	Idiocy	Epileptics Maniacs-Depressives	Paranoics Schizophrenics	Dementia Praecox	
Sex	Incest (The Wälsungs)	Romantic Adultery. Marriage. (Tristan)	Sophisticated Adultery (Figaro)	Promiscuity (Don Giovanni)	
Religion	Blind Superstition (Animism)	Pantheism. Faith Catholicism Protestantism Deism. Twisting Mysticism Quietism.	Legalism. Rationalism Dogmatism	Lucid Cynicism (Logical Positivism)	
Politics	Tyranny (Fascism)	Feudal Aristocracy	Constitutional Capitalism	Anarchy (Economic breakdown or class-war)	
Political Slogans	Fraternity	Justice		Liberty	
Literary types	Odysseus	Don Quixote		Hamlet. Iago	
	The Flying Dutchman The Pirate. Ishmael	The Beggar (Der Leiermann) The Idiot (Dostoevsky) Don Juan (Byron)		Stavrogin Outlaws	
Movie Types	The Sailor. S.A. The Vamp	The Comic hero Marx Bros. Chaplain			

The Journey of the proud concept inward to the sea
Purgatorial
Dissolution of Pride

Purgatory

Fertilising the waste land
Draining the Swamp

Purgatory
Conscious
The journey of the corrupt body close to the desert (Purgation) and Dissication. Wit
Draining the Sea

The Island → ← The Rose Garden
The City of God
↓
Eden = The World = Paradise

THE CAMPUS ON THE HILL

W. D. Snodgrass

Up the reputable walks of old established trees
They stalk, children of the *nouveaux riches*; chimes
Of the tall Clock Tower drench their heads in blessing:
"I don't wanna play at your house;
I don't like you any more."
My house stands opposite, on the other hill,
Among meadows, with the orchard fences down and falling;
Deer come almost to the door.
You cannot see it, even in this clearest morning.
White birds hang in the air between
Over the garbage landfill and those homes thereto adjacent,
Hovering slowly, turning, settling down
Like the flakes sifting imperceptibly onto the little town
In a waterball of glass.
And yet, this morning, beyond this quiet scene,
The floating birds, the backyards of the poor,
Beyond the shopping plaza, the dead canal, the hillside lying tilted in the air,
Tomorrow has broken out today:
Riot in Algeria, in Cyprus, in Alabama;
Aged in wrong, the empires are declining,
And China gathers, soundlessly, like evidence.
What shall I say to the young on such a morning?—
Mind is the one salvation?—also grammar?—
No; my little ones lean not toward revolt. They
Are the Whites, the vaguely furiously driven, who resist
Their souls with such passivity
As would make Quakers swear. All day, dear Lord, all day
They wear their godhead lightly.
They look out from their hill and say,
To themselves, "We have nowhere to go but down;
The great destination is to stay."
Surely the nations will be reasonable;
They look at the world—don't they?—the world's way?
The clock just now has nothing more to say.

146

SOUTHERN MANSION

Arna Bontemps

Poplars are standing there still as death
And ghosts of dead men
Meet their ladies walking
Two by two beneath the shade
And standing on the marble steps.

There is a sound of music echoing
Through the open door
And in the field there is
Another sound tinkling in the cotton:
Chains of bondmen dragging on the ground.

The years go back with an iron clank,
A hand is on the gate,
A dry leaf trembles on the wall.
Ghosts are walking.
They have broken roses down
And poplars stand there still as death.

*Belle Grove, White Castle, Louisiana.
Photograph, n.d. Built in 1857 and classical in design,
this plantation once had seventy-five grand rooms.
Library of Congress*

THE FROST IN THE CORN

Robert McAlmon

The corn has stood ripe on the stalks for months.
I do feel bitter when father blames me
that it is not harvested. I had the silo builded
and for all his protest he knows it's a good investment.
The corn could rest now in yellow ears in the crib
had he had the help pick while I was away buying cattle.

That was not his way ever though.
He found little things to busy him.

Father is old, not strong, and never was practical.
I will get the corn picked as best can be.
Words now will not solve matters.

The corn has stood overlong on the stalk.
Possibly frost has bitten to its center.
Well, what of myself? I have watched life go on
and knew that I was not where I was meant to be.

The sear corn has beauty, as bleak things have.
The green of growing things never touches me
so much as bare dusty stalks above soiled snow.

And there's always the thought
would I be happier elsewhere.

The others have wandered and I have to.
They don't come back but perhaps it's true:
I'm freer than they are; I don't want their lot.
I'm free in not envying though I don't like what I've got.

The Boy by Thomas Hart Benton. 1950. Oil on canvas.
Collection of Jack and Pearl Resnick

JUSTICE DENIED IN MASSACHUSETTS

Edna St. Vincent Millay

Let us abandon then our gardens and go home
And sit in the sitting-room.
Shall the larkspur blossom or the corn grow under this cloud?
Sour to the fruitful seed
Is the cold earth under this cloud,
Fostering quack and weed, we have marched upon but cannot conquer;
We have bent the blades of our hoes against the stalks of them.

Let us go home, and sit in the sitting-room.
Not in our day
Shall the cloud go over and the sun rise as before,
Beneficent upon us
Out of the glittering bay,
And the warm winds be blown inward from the sea
Moving the blades of corn
With a peaceful sound.
Forlorn, forlorn,
Stands the blue hay-rack by the empty mow.
And the petals drop to the ground,
Leaving the tree unfruited.
The sun that warmed our stooping backs and withered the weed uprooted—
We shall not feel it again.
We shall die in darkness, and be buried in the rain.
What from the splendid dead
We have inherited—
Furrows sweet to the grain, and the weed subdued—
See now the slug and the mildew plunder.
Evil does overwhelm
The larkspur and the corn;
We have seen them go under.

Let us sit here, sit still,
Here in the sitting-room until we die;
At the step of Death on the walk, rise and go;
Leaving to our children's children this beautiful doorway,
And this elm,
And a blighted earth to till
With a broken hoe.

Nicola Sacco and Bartolomeo Vanzetti.
Photograph, n.d.
Their execution in Massachusetts,
August 22, 1927,
inspired Edna St. Vincent Millay's poem
on the opposite page.
National Portrait Gallery,
Smithsonian Institution

JAZZ FANTASIA

Carl Sandburg

Drum on your drums, batter on your banjoes,
sob on the long cool winding saxophones.
Go to it, O jazzmen.

Sling your knuckles on the bottoms of the happy
tin pans, let your trombones ooze, and go husha-
husha-hush with the slippery sand-paper.

Moan like an autumn wind high in the lonesome treetops, moan soft like you
wanted somebody terrible, cry like a racing car slipping away from a motor-
cycle cop, bang-bang! you jazzmen, bang altogether drums, traps, banjoes, horns,
tin cans—make two people fight on the top of a stairway and scratch each
other's eyes in a clinch tumbling down the stairs.

Can the rough stuff . . . now a Mississippi steamboat pushes up the night river
with a hoo-hoo-hoo-oo . . . and the green lanterns calling to the high soft stars
. . . a red moon rides on the humps of the low river hills . . . go to it, O jazzmen.

FIRST FIG

Edna St. Vincent Millay

My candle burns at both ends;
    It will not last the night;
But ah, my foes, and oh, my friends—
    It gives a lovely light!

NEWS ITEM

Dorothy Parker

Men seldom make passes
At girls who wear glasses.

REFLECTIONS ON ICE-BREAKING

Ogden Nash

Candy
Is dandy
But liquor
Is quicker.

I DO LOVE MY CHARLIE SO

Zelda Sayre Fitzgerald

I do love my Charlie so.
It nearly drives me wild.
I'm so glad that he's my beau
And I'm his baby child!

King Oliver's Creole Jazz Band.
Photograph by Daguerre, Chicago, about 1923.
William Ransom Hogan Jazz Archive,
Tulane University Library, New Orleans

from
THOUSAND-AND-FIRST SHIP

F. Scott Fitzgerald

There'd be an orchestra
   Bingo! Bango!
Playing for us
   To dance the tango
And people would clap
   When we arose
At her sweet face
   And my new clothes.

Dust jacket by John Held, Jr.
For Tales of the Jazz Age
by F. Scott Fitzgerald,
published September 1922,
by Charles Scribner's Sons, New York

153

LINES WRITTEN FOR GENE KELLY TO DANCE TO

Carl Sandburg

Spring is when the grass turns green and glad.
Spring is when the new grass comes up and says, "Hey, hey!
     Hey, hey!"
Be dizzy now and turn your head upside down and see how
     the world looks upside down.
Be dizzy now and turn a cartwheel, and see the good earth
through a cartwheel.

Tell your feet the alphabet.
Tell your feet the multiplication table.
Tell your feet where to go, and watch 'em go and come back.

Can you dance a question mark?
Can you dance an exclamation point?
Can you dance a couple of commas?
And bring it to a finish with a period?

Can you dance like the wind is pushing you?
Can you dance like you are pushing the wind?
Can you dance with slow wooden heels

     and then change to bright and singing silver heels?
Such nice feet, such good feet.

So long as grass grows and rivers run
Silver lakes like blue porcelain plates
Silver snakes of winding rivers.
You can see 'em on a map.

Why we got geography?
Because we go from place to place. Because the earth used to be flat and had
     four corners, and you could jump off from any of the corners.
But now the earth is not flat any more. Now it is round all over. Now it is a
     globe, a ball, round all over, and we would all fall off it and tumble away
     into space if it wasn't for the magnetic poles. And when you dance it is the
     North Pole or the South Pole pulling on your feet like magnets to keep your
     feet on the earth.
And that's why we got geography.
And it's nice to have it that way.

Why does duh Mississippi River wind and wind?
Why, dat's easy. She wind so she git where she wanna go.
Mississippi, Rappahannock, Punxatawney. Spell out their
    names with your heels.

Where duh towns uh Punxatawney and Mauk Chunk? Why,
    yeanh day's bof in Pennsylvan-ee-eye-ay.
    And dat's why we got geography.

Left foot, tweedle-dum—right foot tweedle-dee, here they go.

When Yankee Doodle come to town, wot wuz he a-ridin' on?
A buffalo? A elephant? A horse?
No, no, no, no. A pony it wuz, a pony.
That's right—
Giddi-ap, Giddi-ap, Giddi-ap, Giddi-ap.
Whoa! Whoa!

Gene Kelly in the film
Singin' in the Rain.
Copyright © 1974 Metro-Goldwyn-Mayer, Inc.
Museum of Modern Art Film Stills Archive, New York

STREET MUSIC

Barbara Angell

Somebody threw away a piano,
left it on the sidewalk
under my window
on Franklin street near Spring Garden.

Early morning on a rainy day
I woke to tinny music
with a wet and muffled undersong.
Never saw the piano player.

When I leaned out to look
the music stopped.
No one anywhere,
only rain falling on the keys
and the gutter singing.

SCHUMANN'S SONATA IN A MINOR   *Celia Thaxter*

The quiet room, the flowers, the perfumed calm,
  The slender crystal vase, where all aflame
The scarlet poppies stand erect and tall,
  Color that burns as if no frost could tame,
The shaded lamplight glowing over all,
  The summer night a dream of warmth and balm.

Outbreaks at once the golden melody,
  "With passionate expression!" Ah, from whence
Comes the enchantment of this potent spell,
  This charm that takes us captive, soul and sense?
The sacred power of music, who shall tell,
  Who find the secret of its mastery?

Lo, in the keen vibration of the air
  Pierced by the sweetness of the violin,
Shaken by thrilling chords and searching notes
  That flood the ivory keys, the flowers begin
To tremble; it is as if some spirit floats
  And breathes upon their beauty unaware.

The stately poppies, proud in stillness, stand
  In silken splendor of superb attire:
Stricken with arrows of melodious sound,
  Their loosened petals fall like flakes of fire;
With waves of music overwhelmed and drowned,
  Solemnly drop their flames on either hand.

So the rich moment dies, and what is left?
  Only a memory sweet, to shut between
Some poem's silent leaves, to find again,
  Perhaps, when winter blasts are howling keen,
And summer's loveliness is spoiled and slain,
  And all the world of light and bloom bereft.

But winter cannot rob the music so!
  Nor time nor fate its subtle power destroy
To bring again the summer's dear caress,
  To wake the heart to youth's unreasoning joy,—
Sound, color, perfume, love, to warm and bless,
  And airs of balm from Paradise that blow.

THE HOUSE WAS QUIET AND
THE WORLD WAS CALM

Wallace Stevens

The house was quiet and the world was calm.
The reader became the book; and summer night

Was like the conscious being of the book.
The house was quiet and the world was calm.

The words were spoken as if there was no book,
Except that the reader leaned above the page,

Wanted to lean, wanted much most to be
The scholar to whom his book is true, to whom

The summer night is like a perfection of thought.
The house was quiet because it had to be.

The quiet was part of the meaning, part of the mind;
The access of perfection to the page.

And the world was calm. The truth in a calm world,
In which there is no other meaning, itself

Is calm, itself is summer and night, itself
Is the reader leaning late and reading there.

The Room of Flowers
by Childe Hassam.
1894. Oil on canvas.
The woman in the painting is poet Celia Thaxter.
Collection Mr. and Mrs. Arthur G. Atschul

THE HOUSE ON BROUGHTON STREET

Mary Ann Larkin

Always it was a summer afternoon
I see my mother climbing the stairs
to the porch
My grandmother waiting
tiny but formidable
She'd been expecting her
the sisters smiling
brothers watching
My mother in her grey crepe
the white gloves she always wore
Her hair and eyes dark
among these fair, freckled people
My father shyly presenting her—
something of his own—
Shuffling, they made room for her
and she took her place among them
and between them
grew something new
Marie, they came to say,
This is Grant's Marie
She seldom spoke
but rested among them
a harbor she'd found

My father gave her a carnelian ring
surrounded by silver hearts
Before Grandma died
she gave my mother the diamond brooch

from Grandpa
My mother brought with her
fabrics that glistened
a touch of velvet
sometimes a feather
They noticed the light
in the rooms where she sat
And even thirty years later
after the lost jobs and the babies
after the mortgages and the wars
what they remembered most
was the way my mother
set aside her gloves

She was buried on Good Friday
There was a blizzard
After the funeral
the youngest uncle
read "Murder in the Cathedral" aloud

I have the carnelian ring now
the diamond brooch
I wear satin when I can
and I am attracted to old houses
where the light passes
across the porch to the windows, making
of the space between, a grace

The Mansard Roof by Edward Hopper.
1923. Watercolor.
The Brooklyn Museum. Museum Collection Fund

YOU WERE WEARING

Kenneth Koch

You were wearing your Edgar Allan Poe printed cotton blouse.
In each divided-up square of the blouse was a picture of Edgar Allan Poe.
Your hair was blonde and you were cute. You asked me, "Do most boys think
      that most girls are bad?"
I smelled the mould of your seaside resort hotel bedroom on your hair held in
      place by a John Greenleaf Whittier clip.
"No," I said, "it's girls who think that boys are bad." Then we read
      Snowbound together
And ran around in an attic, so that a little of the blue enamel was scraped off my
      George Washington, Father of His Country, shoes.

Mother was walking in the living room, her Strauss Waltzes comb in her hair.
We waited for a time and then joined her, only to be served tea in cups painted
      with pictures of Herman Melville
As well as with illustrations from his book *Moby Dick* and from his novella,
      Benito Cereno.
Father came in wearing his Dick Tracy necktie: "How about a drink, everyone?"
I said, "Let's go outside a while." Then we went onto the porch and sat on the
      Abraham Lincoln swing.
You sat on the eyes, mouth, and beard part, and I sat on the knees.
In the yard across the street we saw a snowman holding a garbage can lid
      smashed into a likeness of the mad English king, George the Third.

PICTURE BRIDE

Cathy Song

She was a year younger
than I,
twenty-three when she left Korea.
Did she simply close
the door of her father's house
and walk away. And
was it a long way
through the tailor shops of Pusan
to the wharf where the boat
waited to take her to an island
whose name she had
only recently learned,
on whose shore
a man waited,
turning her photograph
to the light when the lanterns
in the camp outside
Waialua Sugar Mill were lit
and the inside of his room
grew luminous
from the wings of moths
migrating out of the cane stalks?
What things did my grandmother
take with her? And when
she arrived to look
into the face of the stranger
who was her husband,
thirteen years older than she,
did she politely untie
the silk bow of her jacket,
her tent-shaped dress
filling with the dry wind
that blew from the surrounding fields
where the men were burning the cane?

EMBROIDERY
(To the tribal Mien women of West Oakland)

Catherine Nomura Crystal

I go to school in the morning
then come home to
shiny silk threads
curled inside a dark hollow
          of my sewing basket
they rest in reeds still musty
from my uncle's grasses
I pray the smell will never go away
in West Oakland
I sit on a woven stool
The sunlight feels good on my back,
          warms my soul.

Sometimes colored threads
get mixed up with falling leaves
or soar with the birds,
find a tiger's paw imprinted
on a blue mountain side.

I sit by a tall window
with my daughters
flowers of my own garden
my soul yearns for a tropical rain.

I listen
between each stitch to
the rustling of cicadas in the heat
monkeys cooing through the shadow and light
          of the forest
birds multicolored calling out their song.

My hand moves over woven cotton
feeling rough high mountains
I finger the last thread of tropical light
turn on the electricity in my apartment
another day passes
I wait patiently in the darkness
          of the sounds of English.

EVENING MEAL IN THE TWENTIETH CENTURY

John Holmes

How is it I can eat bread here and cut meat,
And in quiet shake salt, speak of the meal,
Pour water, serve my son's small plate?
Here now I love well my wife's gold hair combed,
Her voice, her violin, our books on shelves in another room,
The tall chest shining darkly in supper-light.
I have read tonight
The sudden meaningless foreign violent death
Of a nation we both loved, hope
For a country not ours killed. But blacker than print:
For the million people no house now. For me
A new hurt to the old health of the heart once more:
That sore, that heavy, that dull and I think now incurable
Pain:
Seeing love hated, seeing real death,
Knowing evil alive I was taught was conquered.
How shall I cut this bread gladly, unless more share
The day's meals I earn?
Or offer my wife meat from our fire, our fortune?
It should not have taken me so long to learn.
But how can I speak aloud at my own table tonight
And not curse my own food, not cry out death,
And not frighten my young son?

THE SLEEPING

Lynn Emanuel

I have imagined all this:
in 1940 my parents were in love
and living in the loft on West 10th
above Mark Rothko who painted cabbage roses
on their bedroom walls the night they got married.

I can guess why he did it.
My mother's hair was the color of yellow apples
and she wore a black velvet hat with her pajamas.

I was not born yet. I was remote as starlight.
It is hard for me to imagine that
my parents made love in a roomful of roses
and I wasn't there.

But now I am. My mother is blushing.
This is the wonderful thing about art.
It can bring back the dead. It can wake the sleeping
as it might have late that night
when my father and mother made love above Rothko
who lay in the dark thinking *Roses, Roses, Roses*.

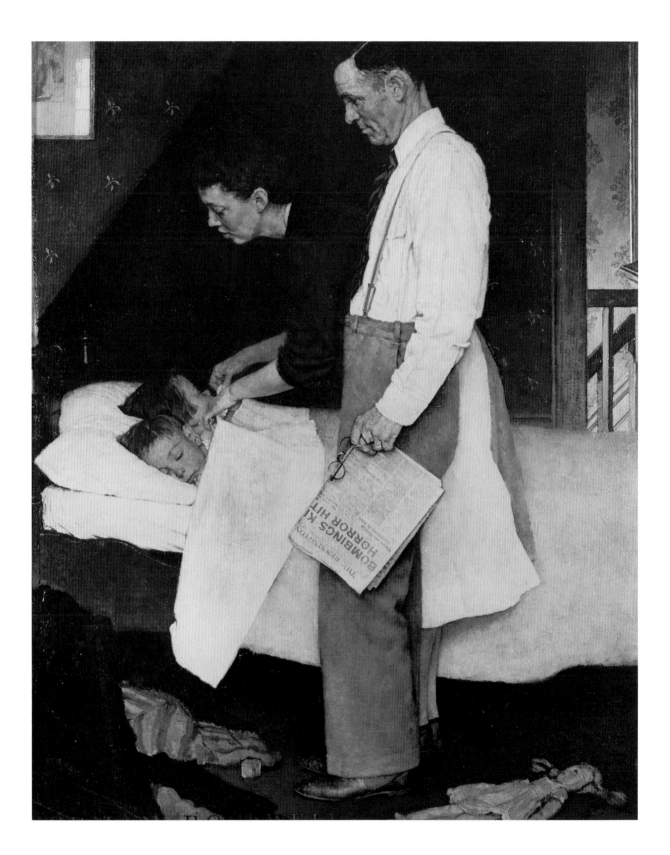

Freedom from Fear *by Norman Rockwell. 1943.*
Oil painting for poster.
Copyright 1943 Estate of Norman Rockwell

COME ON IN, THE SENILITY IS FINE

Ogden Nash

People live forever in Jacksonville and St. Petersburg and Tampa,
But you don't have to live forever to become a grampa.
The entrance requirements for grampahood are comparatively mild,
You only have to live until your child has a child.
From that point on you start looking both ways over your shoulder,
Because sometimes you feel thirty years younger and sometimes thirty
      years older.
Now you begin to realize who it was that reached the height of imbecility,
It was whoever said that grandparents have all the fun and none of
      the responsibility.
This is the most enticing spiderweb of a tarradiddle ever spun,
Because everybody would love to have a baby around who was no responsibility
      and lots of fun,
But I can think of no one but a mooncalf or a gaby
Who would trust their own child to raise a baby.
So you have to personally superintend your grandchild from diapers to pants
      and from bottle to spoon,
Because you know that your own child hasn't sense enough to come in
      out of a typhoon.
You don't have to live forever to become a grampa, but if you do want to
      live forever,
Don't try to be clever;
If you wish to reach the end of the trail with an uncut throat,
Don't go around saying Quote I don't mind being a grampa but I hate being
      married to a gramma Unquote.

OLD-TIME CHILDHOOD IN KENTUCKY

Robert Penn Warren

When I was a boy I saw the world I was in.
I saw it for what it was. Canebrakes with
Track beaten down by bear paw. Tobacco,
In endless rows, the pink inner flesh of black fingers
Crushing to green juice tobacco worms plucked
From a leaf. The great trout,
Motionless, poised in the shadow of his
Enormous creek-boulder.
But the past and the future broke on me, as I got older.

164

Strange, into the past I first grew. I handled the old bullet-mold.
I drew out a saber, touched an old bayonet, I dreamed
Of the death-scream. Old spurs I tried on.
The first great General Jackson had ridden just north to our state
To make a duel legal—or avoid the law.
It was all for honor. He said: "I would have killed him
Even with his hot lead in my heart." This for honor. I longed
To understand. I said the magic word.
I longed to say it aloud, to be heard.

I saw the strategy of Bryce's Crossroads, saw
The disposition of troops at Austerlitz, but knew
It was far away, long ago. I saw
The marks of the old man's stick in the dust, heard
The old voice explaining. His eyes weren't too good,
So I read him books he wanted. Read him
Breasted's *History of Egypt*. Saw years uncoil like a snake.
I built a pyramid with great care. There interred
Pharaoh's splendor and might.
Excavation next summer exposed that glory to man's sight.

At a cave mouth my uncle showed me crinoid stems,
And in limestone skeletons of the fishy form of some creature.
"All once under water," he said, "no saying the millions
Of years." He walked off, the old man still with me. "Grandpa,"
I said, "what do you do, things being like this?" "All you can,"
He said, looking off through treetops, skyward. "Love
Your wife, love your get, keep your word, and
If need arises die for what men die for. There aren't
Many choices.
And remember that truth doesn't always live in the number of voices."

He hobbled away. The woods seemed darker. I stood
In the encroachment of shadow. I shut
My eyes, head thrown back, eyelids black.
I stretched out the arm on each side, and, waterlike,
Wavered from knees and hips, feet yet firm-fixed, it seemed,
On shells, in mud, in sand, in stone, as though
In eons back I grew there in that submarine
Depth and lightlessness, waiting to discover
What I would be, might be, after ages—how many?—had rolled over.

Cover for The Saturday Evening Post,
December 16, 1933,
by Norman Rockwell.
Copyright 1933 Estate of
Norman Rockwell

THE FAVORITE FLOWER

Celia Thaxter

O the warm, sweet, mellow summer noon,
　　The golden calm and the perfumed air,
The chirp of birds and the locust's croon,
　　The rich flowers blossoming still and fair.
The old house lies 'mid the swarming leaves
Steeped in sunshine from porch to eaves,
With doors and windows thrown open wide
To welcome the beauty and bloom outside.

Through the gateway and down the walk,
　　Madge and grandmother, hand in hand
Come with laughter and happy talk,
　　And here by the marigolds stop and stand.
"What a dear old pleasant place it is!"
Cries the little maid in a trance of bliss,
"Never anywhere could be found
So sweet a garden the whole world round!

"Tell me, grandmother, which do you think,
　　Is the dearest flower for you that grows!
The phlox, or the marigold stars that wink,
　　Or the larkspur quaint, or the red, red rose?
Which do you love best, grandmother dear?"
And the old dame smiles in the blue eyes clear—
"Of all the flowers I ever possessed,
I think, my precious, I love you best!"

In the Garden by Mary Cassatt.
1893. Oil on canvas.
The Baltimore Museum of Art: The Cone Collection, formed by
Dr. Claribel Cone and Miss Etta Cone of Baltimore, Maryland.

ROCK 'N' ROLL

Lesley Frost

Then turn on the music, Marcia.
Just snap on the music, Dougie.
Now strike up a dance band, Katie,
I'm dying to try boogie-woogie.

I haven't much use for Beethoven,
It isn't the rhythm I hop to.
Just give me the mambo and tango,
Just find me some jazz or the Bop, too.

For rock 'n' roll's better than Crosby,
Belafonte, Sinatra, King Cole too.
Just give me a tune to start rocking
Just give me a rhythm to roll to.

LONGMOBILE

Shel Silverstein

It's the world's longest car, I swear,
It reaches from Beale Street to Washington Square
And once you get in it
To go where you're going,
You simply get out, 'cause you're *there*.

Longmobile *by Shel Silverstein.*
From A Light in the Attic,
Harper & Row, Publishers, New York, 1974

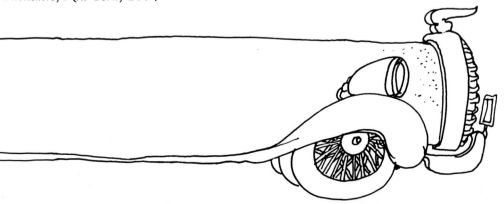

Dancers by Arthur B. Davies.
Oil on canvas.
The Detroit Institute of Arts

I DANCED TO THE RUMBLE OF THE DRUM

Elevena Burbank

```
    i
     d
      a
       n
        c
         e
          d to the rumble of
the drum as my grandmother's
old ceremonial shawl sways
freely
my mind is finally at peace as
my heart  s with every
         p
        a
       e
      l
beat of the drum.
```

BOY BREAKING GLASS

To Marc Crawford—from whom the commission

Gwendolyn Brooks

Whose broken window is a cry of art
(success, that winks aware
as elegance, as a treasonable faith)
is raw: is sonic: is old-eyed première.
Our beautiful flaw and terrible ornament.
Our barbarous and metal little man.

"I shall create! If not a note, a hole.
If not an overture, a desecration."

Full of pepper and light
and Salt and night and cargoes.

"Don't go down the plank
if you see there's no extension.
Each to his grief, each to
his loneliness and fidgety revenge.

Nobody knew where I was and now I am no longer there."

The only sanity is a cup of tea.
The music is in minors.

Each one other
is having different weather.

"It was you, it was you who threw away my name!
And this is everything I have for me."

Who has not Congress, lobster, love, luau,
the Regency Room, the Statue of Liberty,
runs. A sloppy amalgamation.
A mistake.
A cliff.
A hymn, a snare, and an exceeding sun.

DIVORCE

Adam Koehn

It feels like a bear eating me,
It feels like glass breaking,
It feels like anger.

It sounds like trees
falling to the earth,
It sounds like a fire's roar.

It is like a fish
being eaten,
like a building
falling apart.

Two Houses by Walter Stuempfig.
Oil on canvas.
The Corcoran Gallery of Art
Museum purchase,
William A. Clark Fund

Flight

AT THE SAN FRANCISCO AIRPORT

(To J. W., 1954)

Yvor Winters

This is the terminal: the light
Gives perfect vision, false and hard;
The metal glitters, deep and bright.
Great planes are waiting in the yard—
They are already in the night.

And you are here beside me, small,
Contained and fragile, and intent
On things that I but half recall—
Yet going whither you are bent.
I am the past, and that is all.

But you and I in part are one:
The frightened brain, the nervous will,
The knowledge of what must be done,
The passion to acquire the skill
To face that which you dare not shun.

The rain of matter upon sense
Destroys me momently. The score:
There comes what will come. The expense
Is what one thought, and something more—
One's being and intelligence.

This is the terminal, the break.
Beyond this point, on lines of air,
You take the way that you must take;
And I remain in light and stare—
In light, and nothing else, awake.

EVEN—

Anne Morrow Lindbergh

Him that I love I wish to be
Free:

Free as the bare top twigs of tree,
Pushed up out of the fight
Of branches, struggling for the light,
Clear of the darkening pall,
Where shadows fall—
Open to the golden eye
Of sky;

Free as a gull
Alone upon a single shaft of air,
Invisible there,
Where
No man can touch,
No shout can reach,
Meet
No stare;

Free as a spear
Of grass,
Lost in the green
Anonymity
Of a thousand seen
Piercing, row on row,
The crust of earth,
With mirth,
Through to the blue,
Sharing the sun
Although,
Circled, each one,
In his cool sphere
Of dew.

Him that I love, I wish to be
Free—
Even from me.

Anne Morrow Lindbergh
Photograph, n.d.
New York Public Library

A PROJECTION

Reed Whittemore

I wish they would hurry up their trip to Mars,
Those rocket gentlemen.
We have been waiting too long; the fictions of little men
And canals,
And of planting and raising flags and opening markets
For beads, cheap watches, perfume and plastic jewelry—
All these begin to be tedious; what we need now
Is the real thing, a thoroughly bang-up voyage
Of discovery.

Led by Admiral Byrd
In the *Nina, Pinta* and *Santa Maria*
With a crew of one hundred experts
In physics, geology, war and creative writing,
The expedition should sail with a five-year supply of
Pemmican, Jello, Moxie,
Warm woolen socks and jars of Gramma's preserves.

Think of them out there,
An ocean of space before them, using no compass,
Guiding themselves by speculative equations,
Looking,
Looking into the night and thinking now
There are no days, no seasons, time
Is only on watches,
                  and landing on Venus
Through some slight error,
Bearing

Proclamations of friendship,
Declarations of interstellar faith,
Acknowledgments of American supremacy,
And advertising matter.

I wonder,
Out in the pitch of space, having worlds enough,
If the walled-up, balled-up self could from its alley
Sally.
I wish they would make provisions for this,
Those rocket gentlemen.

Mars. A computer-generated false-color exaggeration of the color variation on Mars, showing types of clouds, atmospheric haze, surface forests, and rock materials. Viking 1–4, NASA

from FOR THE FIRST MANNED MOON ORBIT   *James Dickey*

So long
So long as the void
Is hysterical, bolted out, you float on nothing

But procedure alone,

Eating, sleeping like a man
Deprived of the weight of his own
And all humanity in the name

Of a new life
                    and through this, making new
Time slowly, the moon comes.
                                   Its mountains bulge
                 They crack they hold together
         Closer   spreading   smashed crust
Of uncanny rock   ash-glowing   alchemicalizing the sun
         With peace: with the peace of a country
Bombed-out by the universe.
                               You lean back from the great light-
         shattered face   the pale blaze
                 Of God-stone coming

         Close   too close, and the dead seas turn
                 The craters hover   turn
                    Their dark side to kill
                 The radio, and the one voice
         Of earth.

176

You and your computers have brought out
The silence of mountains the animal
Eye has not seen since the earth split,
Since God first found geometry
Would move   move
In mysterious ways. You hang

Mysteriously, pulling   the moon-dark pulling,
And solitude breaks down
Like an electrical system: it is something

Else: nothing is something
Something I am trying

To say O God
Almighty! To come back! To complete the curve   to come back
Singing with procedure   back through the last dark
Of the moon, past the dim ritual
Random stones of oblivion, and through the blinding edge
Of moonlight into the sun

And behold

The blue planet steeped in its dream

Of reality, its calculated vision shaking with
The only love.

WAR

Joseph Langland

When my young brother was killed
By a mute and dusty shell in the thorny brush
Crowning the boulders of the Villa Verde Trail
On the island of Luzon,

I laid my whole dry body down,
Dropping my face like a stone in a green park
On the east banks of the Rhine;

On an airstrip skirting the Seine
His sergeant brother sat like a stick in his barracks
While cracks of fading sunlight
Caged the dusty air;

In the rocky rolling hills west of the Mississippi
His father and mother sat in a simple Norwegian parlor
With a photograph smiling between them on the table
And their hands fallen into their laps
Like sticks and dust;

And still other brothers and sisters,
Linking their arms together,
Walked down the dusty road where once he ran
And into the deep green valley
To sit on the stony banks of the stream he loved
And let the murmuring waters
Wash over their blood-hot feet with a springing
        crown of tears.

ON A PHOTO OF SGT. CIARDI
A YEAR LATER

John Ciardi

The sgt. stands so fluently in leather,
So poster-holstered and so newsreel-jawed
As death's costumed and fashionable brother,
My civil memory is overawed.

Behind him see the circuses of doom
Dance a finale chorus on the sun.
He leans on gun sights, doesn't give a damn
For dice or stripes, and waits to see the fun.

The cameraman whose ornate public eye
Invented that fine bravura look of calm
At murderous clocks hung ticking in the sky
Palmed the deception off without a qualm.

Even the camera, focused and exact
To a two dimensional conclusion,
Uttered its formula of physical fact
Only to lend data to illusion.

The camera always lies. By a law of perception
The obvious surface is always an optical ruse.
The leather was living tissue in its own dimension,
The holsters held benzedrine tablets, the guns were no use.

The careful slouch and dangling cigarette
Were always superstitious as Amen.
The shadow under the shadow is never caught:
The camera photographs the cameraman.

Raising the flag on Mount Suribachi, Iwo Jima.
Photograph by Joe Rosenthal.
Left to right: Private First Class Ira H. Hayes;
Private First Class Franklin R. Sousley, killed in action;
Sergeant Michael Strank, killed in action;
Pharmacist Mate 2/C John H. Bradley;
Private First Class Rene A. Cagnon
and Corporal Harlon H. Block, killed in action.
Department of Defense Photograph (Marine Corps).
U.S. Naval Institute, Annapolis

Sergeant John Ciardi.
Photograph courtesy
Mrs. John Ciardi

KILROY

Eugene McCarthy

Kilroy is gone,
the word is out,
absent without leave
from Vietnam.

Kilroy
who wrote his name
in every can
from Poland to Japan
and places in between
like Sheboygan and Racine
is gone
absent without leave
from Vietnam.

Kilroy
who kept the dice
and stole the ice
out of the BOQ
Kilroy
whose name was good
on every IOU
in World War II
and even in Korea
is gone
absent without leave
from Vietnam.

Kilroy
the unknown soldier
who was the first to land
the last to leave,
with his own hand
has taken his good name
from all the walls
and toilet stalls.
Kilroy
whose name around the world
was like the flag unfurled
has run it down
and left Saigon
and the Mekong
without a hero or a song
and gone
absent without leave
from Vietnam.

ODE FOR THE AMERICAN DEAD IN ASIA

Thomas McGrath

1.
God love you now, if no one else will ever,
Corpse in the paddy, or dead on a high hill
In the fine and ruinous summer of a war
You never wanted. All your false flags were
Of bravery and ignorance, like grade school maps:
Colors of countries you would never see—
Until that weekend in eternity
When, laughing, well armed, perfectly ready to kill
The world and your brother, the safe commanders sent
You into your future. Oh, dead on a hill,
Dead in a paddy, leeched and tumbled to
A tomb of footnotes. We mourn a changeling: you:
Handselled to poverty and drummed to war
By distinguished masters whom you never knew.

180

And We Remember. *Photograph by A1C Robert B. Baker.*
The Vietnam War Memorial, Washington, D.C.
Department of the Air Force

2.

The bee that spins his metal from the sun,
The shy mole drifting like a miner ghost
Through midnight earth—all happy creatures run
As strict as trains on rails the circuits of
Blind instinct. Happy in your summer follies,
You mined a culture that was mined for war:
The state to mold you, church to bless, and always
The elders to confirm you in your ignorance.
No scholar put your thinking cap on nor
Warned that in dead seas fishes died in schools
Before inventing legs to walk the land.
The rulers stuck a tennis racket in your hand,
An Ark against the flood. In time of change
Courage is not enough: the blind mole dies,
And you on your hill, who did not know the rules.

3.

Wet in the windy counties of the dawn
The lone crow skirls his draggled passage home:
And God (whose sparrows fall aslant his gaze,
Like grace or confetti) blinks and he is gone,
And you are gone. Your scarecrow valor grows
And rusts like early lilac while the rose
Blooms in Dakota and the stock exchange
Flowers. Roses, rents, all things conspire
To crown your death with wreaths of living fire.
And the public mourners come: the politic tear
Is cast in the Forum. But, in another year,
We will mourn you, whose fossil courage fills
The limestone histories: brave: ignorant: amazed:
Dead in the rice paddies, dead on the nameless hills.

PART III

Let America Be America Again

LET AMERICA BE AMERICA AGAIN

Langston Hughes

Let America be America again.
Let it be the dream it used to be.
Let it be the pioneer on the plain
Seeking a home where he himself is free.

(America never was America to me.)

Let America be the dream the dreamers dreamed—
Let it be that great strong land of love
Where never kings connive nor tyrants scheme
That any man be crushed by one above.

(It never was America to me.)

O, let my land be a land where Liberty
Is crowned with no false patriotic wreath,
But opportunity is real, and life is free,
Equality is in the air we breathe.

(There's never been equality for me,
Nor freedom in this "homeland of the free.")

Say who are you that mumbles in the dark?
And who are you that draws your veil across the stars?

I am the poor white, fooled and pushed apart,
I am the Negro bearing slavery's scars.
I am the red man driven from the land,
I am the immigrant clutching the hope I seek—
And finding only the same old stupid plan.
Of dog eat dog, of mighty crush the weak.

I am the young man, full of strength and hope,
Tangled in that ancient endless chain
Of profit, power, gain, of grab the land!
Of grab the gold! Of grab the ways of satisfying need!
Of work the men! Of take the pay!
Of owning everything for one's own greed!

182

Liberty Weekend, Photograph by Scott M. Allen,
First prize, Twenty-sixth Annual Naval and Maritime Photo Contest,
U.S. Naval Institute, Annapolis.
Copyright 1986 Scott M. Allen

I am the farmer, bondsman to the soil.
I am the worker sold to the machine.
I am the Negro, servant to you all.
I am the people, humble, hungry, mean—
Hungry yet today despite the dream.
Beaten yet today—O, Pioneers!
I am the man who never got ahead,
The poorest worker bartered through the years.

Yet I'm the one who dreamt our basic dream
In that Old World while still a serf of kings,
Who dreamt a dream so strong, so brave, so true,
That even yet its mighty daring sings
In every brick and stone, in every furrow turned
That's made America the land it has become.
O, I'm the man who sailed those early seas
In search of what I meant to be my home—
For I'm the one who left dark Ireland's shore,
And Poland's plain, and England's grassy lea,
And torn from Black Africa's strand I came
To build a "homeland of the free."

The free?

Who said the free? Not me?
Surely not me? The millions on relief today?
The millions shot down when we strike?

The millions who have nothing for our pay?
For all the dreams we've dreamed
And all the songs we've sung
And all the hopes we've held
And all the flags we've hung,
The millions who have nothing for our pay—
Except the dream that's almost dead today.

O, let America be America again—
The land that never has been yet—
And yet must be—the land where *every* man is free.
The land that's mine—the poor man's, Indian's, Negro's, ME—
Who made America,
Whose sweat and blood, whose faith and pain,
Whose hand at the foundry, whose plow in the rain,
Must bring back our mighty dream again.

Sure, call me any ugly name you choose—
The steel of freedom does not stain.
From those who live like leeches on the people's lives,
We must take back our land again,
America!

O, yes,
I say it plain,
America never was America to me,
And yet I swear this oath—
America will be!

Out of the rack and ruin of our gangster death,
The rape and rot of graft, and stealth, and lies,
We, the people, must redeem
The land, the mines, the plants, the rivers,
The mountains and the endless plain—
All, all the stretch of these great green states—
And make America again!

PATRIOTIC TOUR AND POSTULATE OF JOY

Robert Penn Warren

Once, once, in Washington,
D.C., in June,
All night—I swear it—a single mockingbird
Sang,
Sang to the Presidential ear,
Wherein it poured
Such criticism and advice as that ear
Had rarely had the privilege to hear.

And sang to every senator
Available,
And some, as sources best informed affirm,
Rose,
Rose with a taste in the throat like bile,
To the bathroom fled
And spat, and faced the mirror there, and while
The bicarb fizzed, stared, feet cold on tile.

And sang to Edgar Hoover, too,
And as it preached
Subversion and all bright disaster, he
Woke;
Woke, then looked at Mom's photo, so heard
No more. But far,
Far off in Arlington, the heroes stirred
And meditated on the message of that bird.

And sang—oh, merciless!—to me,
Who to that place
And to that massive hour had moved, and now
Rose,
Rose naked, and shivered in moonlight, and cried
Out in my need
To know what postulate of joy men have tried
To live by, in sunlight and moonlight, until they died.

SALEM

Robert Lowell

In Salem seasick spindrift drifts or skips
To the canvas flapping on the seaward panes
Until the knitting sailor stabs at ships
Nosing like sheep of Morpheus through his brain's
Asylum. Seaman, seaman, how the draft
Lashes the oily slick about your head,
Beating up whitecaps! Seaman, Charon's raft
Dumps its damned goods into the harbor-bed,—
There sewage sickens the rebellious seas.
Remember, seaman, Salem fishermen
Once hung their nimble fleets on the Great Banks.
Where was it that New England bred the men
Who quartered the Leviathan's fat flanks
And fought the British Lion to his knees?

Crazy Quilt Bed Cover.
Quilt by Celestine Bacheller, about 1850–1900.
Embroidered linen.
Museum of Fine Arts, Boston.
Gift of Mr. and Mrs. Edward J. Healy in memory of Mrs. Charles O'Malley

THE ONE THING THAT CAN SAVE AMERICA

John Ashbery

Is anything central?
Orchards flung out on the land,
Urban forests, rustic plantations, knee-high hills?
Are place names central?
Elm Grove, Adcock Corner, Story Book Farm?
As they concur with a rush at eye level
Beating themselves into eyes which have had enough
Thank you, no more thank you.
And they come on like scenery mingled with darkness
The damp plains, overgrown suburbs,
Places of known civic pride, of civil obscurity.

These are connected to my version of America
But the juice is elsewhere.
This morning as I walked out of your room
After breakfast crosshatched with
Backward and forward glances, backward into light,
Forward into unfamiliar light,
Was it our doing, and was it
The material, the lumber of life, or of lives
We were measuring, counting?
A mood soon to be forgotten
In crossed girders of light, cool downtown shadow
In this morning that has seized us again?

I know that I braid too much my own
Snapped-off perceptions of things as they come to me.
They are private and always will be.
Where then are the private turns of event
Destined to boom later like golden chimes
Released over a city from a highest tower?
The quirky things that happen to me, and I tell you,
And you instantly know what I mean?
What remote orchard reached by winding roads
Hides them? Where are these roots?

188

Poem and
Portrait of John Ashbery
by Larry Rivers. 1977–82.
Acrylic on canvas.
Collection the artist

It is the lumps and trials
That tell us whether we shall be known
And whether our fate can be exemplary, like a star.
All the rest is waiting
For a letter that never arrives,
Day after day, the exasperation
Until finally you have ripped it open not knowing what it is,
The two envelope halves lying on a plate.
The message was wise, and seemingly
Dictated a long time ago.
Its truth is timeless, but its time has still
Not arrived, telling of danger, and the mostly limited
Steps that can be taken against danger
Now and in the future, in cool yards,
In quiet small houses in the country,
Our country, in fenced areas, in cool shady streets.

I AM WAITING

Lawrence Ferlinghetti

I am waiting for my case to come up
and I am waiting
for a rebirth of wonder
and I am waiting for someone
to really discover America
and wail
and I am waiting
for the discovery
of a new symbolic western frontier
and I am waiting
for the American Eagle
to really spread its wings
and straighten up and fly right
and I am waiting
for the Age of Anxiety
to drop dead
and I am waiting
for the war to be fought
which will make the world safe
for anarchy
and I am waiting
for the final withering away
of all governments
and I am perpetually awaiting
a rebirth of wonder

Map by Jasper Johns. 1961
Museum of Modern Art.
Fractional gift of Mr. and Mrs. Robert C. Scull

THE GIFT OUTRIGHT

Robert Frost

The land was ours before we were the land's.
She was our land more than a hundred years
Before we were her people. She was ours
In Massachusetts, in Virginia,
But we were England's, still colonials,
Possessing what we still were unpossessed by,
Possessed by what we now no more possessed.
Something we were withholding made us weak
Until we found out that it was ourselves
We were withholding from our land of living,
And forthwith found salvation in surrender.
Such as we were we gave ourselves outright
(The deed of gift was many deeds of war)
To the land vaguely realizing westward,
But still unstoried, artless, unenhanced,
Such as she was, such as she would become.

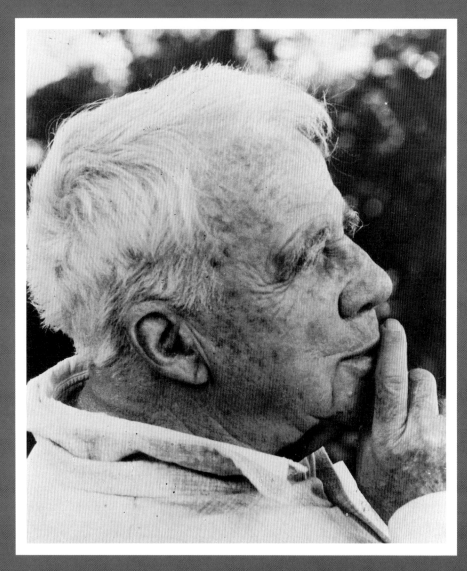

Robert Frost.
Photograph by
David H. Rhinelander.
Library of Congress

LOVE IN AMERICA?

Marianne Moore

Whatever it is, it's a passion—
a benign dementia that should be
engulfing America, fed in a way
   the opposite of the way
in which the Minotaur was fed.
It's a Midas of tenderness;
   from the heart;
nothing else. From one with ability
to bear being misunderstood—
   take the blame, with "nobility
   that is action," identifying itself with
   pioneer unperfunctoriness

   without brazenness or
   bigness of overgrown
   undergrown shallowness.

Whatever it is, let it be without
   affectation.

Yes, yes, yes, *yes*.

Love by Robert Indiana. 1966.
Acrylic on canvas.
Copyright Indianapolis Museum of Art.
Purchased from the James E. Roberts Fund

Biographical Notes

Anna Akhmatova (Anna Andreyevna Govenko) (1874–1946). Russian poet and translator (never visited America).

Barbara Angell (b. 1945). Writer, artist, and teacher who lives in Ohio. Locus of the poem "Street Music" is Philadelphia.

Anonymous. "Dance the Boatman" is a nineteenth-century poem passed along over the years by word of mouth.

John Ashbery (b. 1927). Poet, playwright, and art critic. Awarded the Pulitzer Prize in 1976.

W. H. Auden (1907–1973). Poet and playwright; born in England, became an American citizen in 1946. Taught at Swarthmore College, Pennsylvania, and elsewhere. Awarded the Pulitzer Prize in 1948.

Rosemary Carr Benét (1898–1962). American woman of letters who collaborated with her husband, Stephen, on "Western Wagons" and other poems in *A Book of Americans* (1933).

Stephen Vincent Benét (1898–1943). Poet and storyteller; awarded the Pulitzer Prize in 1929, 1944. John Brown (1800–1859), the subject of his poem, was a leading opponent of slavery in the United States.

George Berkeley (1685–1753). Irish philosopher and Anglican bishop who visited America 1728–31. His dreams of starting a college in Bermuda did not materialize, but the town of Berkeley, California, was later named after him.

Duane BigEagle (b. 1946). Poet and artist who lives on a sheep ranch in northern California; he is the grandson of an Osage Indian.

Elizabeth Bishop (1911–1979). New England poet who frequently lectured at Harvard University, Cambridge, Massachusetts, and elsewhere. Awarded the Pulitzer Prize in 1956, the National Book Award in 1970, and many other distinctions.

Robert Bly (b. 1926). Poet and translator who lives in Minnesota. Won the National Book Award in 1968.

Louise Bogan (1897–1970). Professor and poet who received many awards for her work.

Arna Bontemps (1902–1973). Prolific writer on black history and related topics; librarian at Fisk University, Nashville, Tennessee, for many years.

Philip Booth (b. 1925). Poet with a special interest in the New England coast. Subject of his poem "Marin" is American painter John Marin (1872–1953).

Margie Belle Boswell (1875–1952). Texas poet and newspaper columnist who was well known for her epigrams.

Hugh Henry Brackenridge (1748–1816). Patriot, poet, and man of letters. He and Philip Freneau (1752–1832) presented their poem about "the rising glory of America" at their graduation from Nassau Hall (now Princeton University, New Jersey) in 1771.

Anne Bradstreet (c. 1612–1672). English Puritan and American poet whose husband was governor of the Massachusetts Bay Colony.

Gwendolyn Brooks (b. 1917). Poet who was awarded the Pulitzer Prize in 1950. Library of Congress poet in residence 1985–86.

William Cullen Bryant (1794–1878). Poet, newspaper editor, and lawyer. He was a close friend of Thomas Cole (1801–1848). Asher B. Durand's painting *Kindred Spirits* shows them in the Adirondack mountains, New York.

Elevena Burbank (b. 1956). A student at Navajo Community College, Tsaile, Arizona, when her poem was first published.

Robert Carson (b. 1945). Poet and editor of an anthology about the San Francisco waterfront.

Willa Cather (1873–1947). Poet and novelist raised in Nebraska, which she described in *My Antonia* (1918) and other works.

Arthur Chapman (1873–1935). Poet, novelist, and newspaper editor in Colorado.

John Ciardi (1916–1986). Poet, editor, and teacher who served in the U.S. Air Force during World War II; well known for his translations of Dante.

Thomas Cole (1801–1848). English-born American artist; leader of the Hudson River School of painting.

Hart Crane (1899–1932). Poet born in Garretsville, Ohio, who focused on the Brooklyn Bridge as a symbol of American life.

Stephen Crane (1871–1900). Novelist, poet, and war correspondent; best known for *The Red Badge of Courage* (1895).

Vesta Pierce Crawford (1899–1983). Poet and woman of letters who wrote much about her native state of Utah.

Catherine Nomura Crystal (b. 1943). Japanese-American poet who teaches English to Southeast Asian refugees in Oakland, California. Mien, mentioned in the dedication to "Embroidery," is in Laos.

James Dickey (b. 1923). Poet and novelist, best known for *Deliverance* (1970). Professor of English and writer in residence, University of South Carolina, Columbia.

Emily Dickinson (1830–1886). Reclusive poet who lived in Amherst, Massachusetts; her work was published posthumously.

Michael Drayton (1563–1631). English poet (never visited America). "To the Virginian Voyage" was published in London.

T. S. Eliot (1888–1965). Poet, playwright, and critic; born in the United States, became a British citizen in 1927. Awarded the Nobel Prize in 1948.

Lynn Emanuel (b. 1949). Poet who teaches at the University of Pittsburgh.

Ralph Waldo Emerson (1803–1882). New England philosopher and poet. "Concord Hymn" was presented July 1837 at the dedication of the monument commemorating the battles of Lexington and Concord, 1775.

Lawrence Ferlinghetti (b. 1919). Poet, publisher, and adventurer; served as U.S. Navy officer in World War II.

F. Scott Fitzgerald (1896–1940). Best known for his novel *The Great Gatsby* (1925); gave the name "Jazz Age" to the 1920s.

Robert Fitzgerald (1910–1985). Poet and translator who taught at Harvard University, Cambridge, Massachusetts, for many years.

Zelda Sayre Fitzgerald (1900–1948). Writer and artist who symbolized the Roaring Twenties for many people.

Curley N. Fletcher. American cowboy who wrote poems and songs during the 1920s and 30s.

Benjamin Franklin (1706–1790). Scientist, philosopher, and statesman; he wrote "The Mother Country" on the eve of the American Revolution.

John Charles Frémont (1813–1890). Army officer during the Mexican War, explorer, senator, territorial governor, and candidate for president of the United States, 1856.

Philip Freneau (1752–1832). Poet, journalist, and privateer held prisoner by the British, 1779–80. Freneau and Hugh Henry Brackenridge (1748–1816) presented their poem about "the rising glory of America" at their graduation from Nassau Hall (now Princeton University, New Jersey) in 1771.

Lesley Frost (1899–1983). Poet and teacher whose father, Robert Frost, wrote to her in 1963: "You have found a way with the young."

Robert Frost (1874–1963). One of America's most popular and widely read poets; awarded the Pulitzer Prize in 1924, 1931, 1937, and 1943.

Allen Ginsberg (b. 1926). Poet of the Beat Generation and social activist; known for *Howl, and Other Poems* (1956). Won the National Book Award in 1974.

Johann Wolfgang von Goethe (1749–1832). German poet and dramatist (never visited America).

Rebecca Gonzales. Hispanic-American poet who lives in Texas and writes about the lives of her people.

Linda Gregg (b. 1942). Poet and teacher; awarded a fellowship from the Guggenheim Foundation.

O. B. Hardison, Jr. (b. 1928). Poet and former director of the Folger Shakespeare Library, Washington, D.C. Locus of his poem "Marina" is the Outer Banks of North Carolina.

Thomas Hardy (1840–1928). English poet and novelist (never visited America). Best known for *The Return of the Native* (1878).

Bret Harte (1836–1902) Journalist, writer, and poet whose early stories about the American West brought him fame and fortune. His poem "Chicago" refers to the devastating fire of October 1871.

Ernest Hemingway (1899–1961). Adventurer and writer whose novels include *A Farewell to Arms* (1929). Awarded the Nobel Prize for literature in 1954.

Robert Hillyer (1895–1961). Poet and professor at Harvard University, Cambridge, Massachusetts; awarded the Pulitzer Prize in 1934.

John Hollander (b. 1929). Poet, musician, and professor at Yale University, New Haven, Connecticut.

John Holmes (1904–1962). Poet and essayist who taught at Tufts University, Medford, Massachusetts.

Oliver Wendell Holmes (1809–1894). Poet, physician, and professor. Following the publication of his poem "Old Ironsides," the ship (U.S.S. *Constitution*) was saved from destruction and restored; she is docked in Boston.

Langston Hughes (1902–1967). Adventurer, novelist, and poet; a major figure of the Negro Renaissance of the 1920s.

Robinson Jeffers (1887–1962). Poet who celebrated California's Big Sur and other scenic places.

Donald Justice (b. 1925). Poet who teaches at the University of Florida; awarded the Pulitzer Prize in 1980.

X. J. Kennedy (b. 1929). Poet, editor, and essayist. Locus of his poem "In a Prominent Bar in Secaucus One Day" is a small New Jersey community near New York City.

Francis Scott Key (1779–1843). American lawyer who observed the British attack on Fort McHenry, Baltimore harbor, September 13–14, 1814. Key wrote his poem on the back of an envelope that night. It became famous and later was set to music.

Sarah Kemble Knight (1666–1727). Boston schoolteacher who had Benjamin Franklin as a student. Her poem "Resentments . . ." was composed during a trip to New York in 1704.

Kenneth Koch (b. 1925). Poet, novelist, and playwright who teaches at Columbia University, New York City.

Adam Koehn (b. 1974). A sixth-grade student in Mineral, California, when his poem "Divorce" was selected for publication in a statewide anthology.

Kendra Kopelke (b. 1957). Her poem "Eager Street" describes a section of Baltimore where traditionally the stone front steps of the row houses are scrubbed white every morning.

Joseph Langland (b. 1917). Poet who served in the U.S. Army 1942–46. Taught English for many years at the University of Massachusetts.

Mary Ann Larkin (b. 1945). Poet and teacher who lives in Washington, D.C. Locus of her poems "Riding on a Streetcar with My Father" and "The House on Broughton Street" is Pittsburgh, Pennsylvania.

Richmond Lattimore (1906–1984). Poet and translator who taught at Bryn Mawr College, Pennsylvania, for many years. Locus of his poem "Max Schmitt in a Single Scull" is Philadelphia; the subject is a Thomas Eakins (1844–1916) painting.

Emma Lazarus (1849–1887). Poet, essayist, and philanthropist who was concerned with the problems of Jewish immigrants in America. Her poem "The New Colossus" celebrates the Statue of Liberty.

Anne Morrow Lindbergh (b. 1907). Poet, aviator, and explorer. Her poem "Even—" is about her husband, Charles (1902—1974), who gained worldwide fame for making the first solo nonstop transatlantic flight, in 1927.

Henry Wadsworth Longfellow (1807–1882). New England poet and professor whose long verse narratives contributed to an American mythology.

Amy Lowell (1874–1925). Poet and critic who lived in Brookline, Massachusetts; awarded the Pulitzer Prize in 1926.

James Russell Lowell (1819–1891). New England poet, essayist, and diplomat. His ode to George Washington was considered in his time the best poem written by an American.

Robert Lowell (1917–1977). Poet and translator; awarded the Pulitzer Prize in 1947, the National Book Award in 1960, and many other honors.

Robert McAlmon (1896–1956). American poet and novelist who was the first publisher of Ernest Hemingway; lived in France during the 1920s and wrote about the "lost generation."

Eugene J. McCarthy (b. 1916). Writer and politician who represented Minnesota in the U.S. House of Representatives, 1949–58, and the U.S. Senate, 1958–70. During World War II, American soldiers overseas would mark the places they passed through by writing "Kilroy was here."

Thomas McGrath (b. 1916). Poet and novelist who served in the U.S. Air Force, 1943–46; professor emeritus of English, Moorhead University, Minnesota.

Dolley Madison (1768–1849). American hostess and poet. Her husband, James, was president of the United States, 1809–17. The subject of her poem "Lafayette" is the Marquis de Lafayette (1757–1834), a commander of American troops during the Revolution who symbolized French aid to the colonies.

Cotton Mather (1663–1728). Puritan clergyman and writer who lived in Boston. His poem "Go then, my Dove, but now no longer mine" is about the death of his third wife, Abigail, in November 1702.

Herman Melville (1819–1891). Novelist and poet best known for his stories of adventure at sea, including *Moby Dick* (1851).

Edna St. Vincent Millay (1892–1950). Poet and playwright; awarded the Pulitzer Prize in 1923. Her poem "To Inez Milholland" refers to the statue of Lucretia Mott, Susan B. Anthony, and Elizabeth Cady Stanton, located in the United States Capitol. "Justice Denied in Massachusetts" refers to the anarchists Nicola Sacco and Bartolomeo Vanzetti, immigrants executed August 22, 1927, for murder, but thought to be victims of injustice sentenced to death for their politics.

Clement Moore (1779–1863). Writer and scholar who taught at the General Theological Seminary, New York. His poem "The Night Before Christmas," beloved by generations of readers, was first published in 1823.

Marianne Moore (1887–1972). Poet, literary critic, and editor, awarded many honors, including both the Pulitzer Prize and the National Book Award in 1952.

Ogden Nash (1902–1971). Writer and humorist. "Ice-breaking" is American slang for becoming acquainted.

Dorothy Parker (1893–1967). Writer and humorist known for her sharp, sophisticated wit.

Sylvia Plath (1932–1963). Poet and novelist who was posthumously awarded the Pulitzer Prize in 1981.

Edgar Allan Poe (1809–1849). American poet, journalist, and short-story writer; best known for his tales of imagination and horror, including "The Murders in the Rue Morgue" (1841).

Ezra Pound (1885–1972). Poet, critic, editor, and translator who lived abroad for many years. His poem "To Whistler, American" refers to James Abbott McNeill Whistler (1834–1903), American painter whose work was seen by Pound at the Tate Gallery, London, 1911.

Paul Revere (1735–1818). Boston patriot, engraver, and silversmith. His poem "Unhappy Boston" is about the Boston Massacre of March 5, 1770. He made his famous ride the night of April 18, 1775.

Adrienne Rich (b. 1929). Poet, critic, and professor who received the National Book Award in 1974 and many other honors.

Edwin Arlington Robinson (1869–1935). Poet who rivaled Robert Frost in popularity earlier in this century; awarded the Pulitzer Prize in 1922, 1925, and 1928.

Muriel Rukeyser (1913–1980). Social activist, teacher, poet, and woman of letters who received many awards for her writing.

Luis Omar Salinas (b. 1937). Hispanic-American poet who lives in California.

Carl Sandburg (1878–1967). Poet and biographer of Abraham Lincoln; awarded the Pulitzer Prize in 1930, 1951 (poetry), and 1940 (history).

Alan Seeger (1888–1916). American poet who joined the French Foreign Legion at the beginning of World War I and died in action in France.

Henricus Selyns (1636–1701). Dutch Reformed clergyman who came to Breukelen, now Brooklyn, New York, in 1660.

Karl Shapiro (b. 1913). Poet, editor, and essayist who teaches at the University of California, Davis. Awarded the Pulitzer Prize in 1945.

Percy Bysshe Shelley (1792–1822). English Romantic poet (never visited America).

Shel Silverstein (b. 1932). Cartoonist, poet, and author of children's books. Best known for *The Giving Tree* (1964) and *A Light in the Attic* (1982).

Samuel Francis Smith (1808–1895). New England clergyman and poet. Wrote "America" in less than half an hour while compiling a book of songs for schoolchildren.

Thomas Smith. Little is known of him apart from the self-portrait that he painted about 1690.

William Jay Smith (b. 1918). Poet and professor; served in the U.S. Navy and in the Vermont legislature.

W. D. Snodgrass (b. 1926). Poet and teacher at Syracuse University, New York, and elsewhere. Awarded the Pulitzer Prize in 1960.

Cathy Song (b. 1955). Poet who lives and teaches in Hawaii; her poem "Picture Bride" describes the arrival there, from Korea, of her grandmother as a young woman.

Stephen Spender (b. 1909). English poet, critic, and lecturer at many universities; knighted in 1983.

Marcia Spriggs (b. 1954). A student at Marygrove College, Detroit, Michigan, when "Poem for Arizona" was first published.

Gertrude Stein (1874–1946). American writer, woman of letters, and art collector who lived in Paris for many years.

Wallace Stevens (1879–1955). Poet and insurance executive who lived in Connecticut; won the National Book Award in 1950 and the Pulitzer Prize in 1955.

Robert Louis Stevenson (1850–1894). Scottish novelist and poet; visited America in 1879–80 and in 1887–88. Best known for his novel *Treasure Island* (1883).

Charles Sullivan (b. 1933). Poet and professor of public administration at Southeastern University, Washington, D.C. Locus of his poem "Nights along the River" is Maryland's Eastern Shore.

Arthur Sze (b. 1950). Chinese-American poet who specializes in the American Southwest.

Allen Tate (1899–1979). Poet, critic, and editor; born in Kentucky, he lectured at many institutions here and abroad, including New York University and Oxford, England.

William Makepeace Thackeray (1811–1863). English novelist and poet; he based his account of Pocahontas on Captain John Smith's book *The General Historie of Virginia* (1624).

Celia Thaxter (1835–1894). New England writer who published several books combining her poetry with the art of Childe Hassam (1859–1935) and other artists.

E. L. Thayer (1863–1940). Journalist and editor. His poem "Casey at the Bat," first published in 1888, gave rise to many imitations, variations, and replies.

Henry David Thoreau (1817–1862). Philosopher and writer; best known for *Walden* (1854).

Mark Twain (Samuel Clemens) (1835–1910). Humorist and novelist; best known for *The Adventures of Tom Sawyer* (1876).

Henry Van Dyke (1852–1933). Presbyterian clergyman and prolific writer; served as United States minister to the Netherlands and Luxembourg, 1913–17.

Robert Penn Warren (b. 1905). Poet, novelist, and professor at Yale University, New Haven, Connecticut, for many years. Awarded Pulitzer Prizes in 1946, 1958, and 1979. American Poet Laureate, 1986–87.

James Welch (b. 1940). Native American poet and novelist who describes life among the Blackfoot Indians of Montana.

Phillis Wheatley (c. 1753–1784). Born in Senegal, West Africa, and brought to Boston as a slave; she gained freedom and fame as a poet there and in London.

Walt Whitman (1819–1892). Poet and journalist. During the Civil War he visited hospitals to help the wounded. His popular book of poetry, *Leaves of Grass*, was first published in 1855.

Reed Whittemore (b. 1919). Poet who served in the U.S. Air Force during World War II. Professor of English at the University of Maryland.

John Greenleaf Whittier (1807–1892). New England poet whose nostalgic accounts of American life became very popular.

Richard Wilbur (b. 1921). Poet, songwriter, translator, and professor; writer in residence at Smith College, Northampton, Massachusetts, since 1977. Awarded the Pulitzer Prize in 1957 and many other honors. American Poet Laureate, 1987–88.

William Carlos Williams (1883–1963). Physician and poet who lived and worked in Rutherford, New Jersey. His poem "The Great Figure" inspired a painting by Charles Demuth (1883–1935). Awarded the Pulitzer Prize in 1963.

Winnebago. A tribe of North American Indians in Wisconsin.

Yvor Winters (1900–1968). Poet and critic; taught at Stanford University, Palo Alto, California, for many years.

William Wordsworth (1770–1850). English Romantic poet (never visited America). He had a strong interest in revolution and democracy.

Valerie Worth (b. 1933). Writes poetry and fiction for children.

Acknowledgments

Index of Poems

204

Index of Poets

Index of Artists